HISTORIANS AT WORK

What Did the Declaration Declare?

HISTORIANS AT WORK

Advisory Editor
Edward Countryman, Southern Methodist University

HISTORIANS AT WORK

What Did the Declaration Declare?

Readings Selected and Introduced by

Joseph J. Ellis

Mount Holyoke College

Selections by

Dumas Malone

Carl Becker

Garry Wills

Joseph J. Ellis

Pauline Maier

Bedford / St. Martin's   *Boston* ≋ *New York*

For Bedford/St. Martin's

History Editor: Katherine E. Kurzman
Production Supervisor: Catherine Hetmansky
Marketing Manager: Charles Cavaliere
Editorial Assistant: Gretchen Boger
Copyeditor: Cynthia Benn
Text Design: Claire Seng-Niemoeller
Cover Design: Peter Blaiwas
Cover Art: Original revised manuscript of *The Declaration of Independence,* Thomas Jefferson. Library of Congress.
Composition: G&S Typesetters, Inc.
Printing and Binding: Haddon Craftsmen, Inc.

President: Charles H. Christensen
Editorial Director: Joan E. Feinberg
Director of Editing, Design, and Production: Marcia Cohen
Managing Editor: Elizabeth M. Schaaf

Library of Congress Catalog Card Number: 98–87528

3   2   1   0   9
f   e   d   c   b   a

For information, write: Bedford/St. Martin's, 75 Arlington Street, Boston, MA 02116 (617-426-7440)

ISBN: 0–312–19063–8

Acknowledgments

Page 2: Painting of Thomas Jefferson (1800) by Rembrandt Peale. The White House Collection. Copyright White House Historical Association.

CARL BECKER, from *The Declaration of Independence: A Study in the History of Political Ideas* by Carl Becker. Copyright © 1922, 1942, renewed 1970 by Carl Becker. Reprinted by permission of Alfred A. Knopf, Inc.

JOSEPH J. ELLIS, from *American Sphinx: The Character of Thomas Jefferson* by Joseph J. Ellis. Copyright © 1997 by Joseph J. Ellis. Reprinted by permission of Alfred A. Knopf, Inc.

PAULINE MAIER, from *American Scripture: Making the Declaration of Independence* by Pauline Maier. Copyright © 1997 by Pauline Maier. Reprinted by permission of Alfred A. Knopf, Inc.

DUMAS MALONE, from *Jefferson the Virginian* by Dumas Malone. Copyright © 1948 by Dumas Malone; renewed 1976 by Dumas Malone. Reprinted by permission of Little, Brown & Company.

GARRY WILLS, from *Inventing America: Jefferson's Declaration of Independence* by Garry Wills. Copyright © 1978 by Garry Wills. Used by permission of Doubleday, a division of Random House, Inc.

Foreword

The short, inexpensive, and tightly focused books in the Historians at Work series set out to show students what historians do by turning closed specialist debate into an open discussion about important and interesting historical problems. These volumes invite students to confront the issues historians grapple with while providing enough support so that students can form their own opinions and join the debate. The books convey the intellectual excitement of "doing history" that should be at the core of any undergraduate study of the discipline. Each volume starts with a contemporary historical question that is posed in the book's title. The question focuses on either an important historical document (the Declaration of Independence, the Emancipation Proclamation) or a major problem or event (the beginnings of American slavery, the Pueblo Revolt of 1680) in American history. An introduction supplies the basic historical context students need and then traces the ongoing debate among historians, showing both how old questions have yielded new answers and how new questions have arisen. Following this two-part introduction are four or five interpretive selections by top scholars, reprinted in their entirety from journals and books, including endnotes. Each selection is either a very recent piece or a classic argument that is still in play and is headed by a question that relates it to the book's core problem. Volumes that focus on a document reprint it in the opening materials so that students can read arguments alongside the evidence and reasoning on which they rest.

One purpose of these books is to show students that they *can* engage with sophisticated writing and arguments. To help them do so, each selection includes apparatus that provides context for engaged reading and critical thinking. An informative headnote introduces the angle of inquiry that the reading explores and closes with Questions for a Closer Reading, which invite students to probe the selection's assumptions, evidence, and argument. At the end of the book, Making Connections questions offer students ways to read the essays against one another, showing how interesting problems emerge from the debate. Suggestions for Further Reading conclude each book, pointing interested students toward relevant materials for extended study.

Historical discourse is rarely a matter of simple opposition. These volumes show how ideas develop and how answers change, as minor themes turn into major considerations. The Historians at Work volumes bring together thoughtful statements in an ongoing conversation about topics that continue to engender debate, drawing students into the historical discussion with enough context and support to participate themselves. These books aim to show how serious scholars have made sense of the past and why what they do is both enjoyable and worthwhile.

EDWARD COUNTRYMAN

Preface

Perhaps the most self-evident truth in American history is that the Declaration of Independence is one of our founding documents and classic texts. A classic, by definition, contains seminal insights; and by implication an American classic contains wisdom about our history that each generation needs to reexamine and rediscover for itself. Few documents have been rediscovered and reinterpreted with the ferocity of the Declaration, which along with the United States Constitution represents a veritable seedbed of contested truths that make special claims on our attention.

The purpose of this volume is to permit students to engage this classic text with the aid of several historians who have each grappled with its meaning and offered distinctive interpretations of their own. While there is considerable overlap and agreement among the historians chosen, there is also a running argument going on among them. Abraham Lincoln once said that America was founded on a proposition, which in fact was contained within one paragraph of the Declaration. A more accurate way to put it is that America was founded on an argument about what that proposition means. The selections included here are designed to bring this generation of students into that argument and, to paraphrase Carl Becker, to make each student his or her own historian.

Three criteria have guided my choice of the selections: first the focus should be on the meaning of the Declaration at the time of its creation in 1776, not on the multiple meanings subsequent generations found in it later; second, the selections should represent a range of interpretive possibilities that capture the major perspectives historians have assumed toward the language and political philosophy of the Declaration; third, the prose style of each selection should be accessible to aspiring historians, should wear its learning lightly, should combine intellectual sophistication with an instinct for its audience of readers.

Acknowledgments

Let me thank Andrew Burstein, Pauline Maier, and Peter Onuf for the benefit of their opinions about the scholarship from which the selections were made. Jack Rakove, Susan Curtis, and an anonymous reviewer offered useful criticisms of an early draft of the introductory essay and commented helpfully on the choice of the selections.

The editorial staff at Bedford/St. Martin's moved the manuscript through the inevitable phases of composition with professional skill. A special thanks is owed Katherine Kurzman, who handled my periodic outbursts and declarations of authorial independence with the same kind of patience, humor, and common sense that Benjamin Franklin exhibited while the Continental Congress was revising Jefferson's draft of the Declaration.

JOSEPH J. ELLIS

A Note for Students

Every piece of written history starts when somebody becomes curious and asks questions. The very first problem is who, or what, to study. A historian might ask an old question yet again, after deciding that existing answers are not good enough. But brand-new questions can emerge about old, familiar topics, particularly in light of new findings or directions in research, such as the rise of women's history in the late 1970s.

In one sense history is all that happened in the past. In another it is the universe of potential evidence that the past has bequeathed. But written history does not exist until a historian collects and probes that evidence (*research*), makes sense of it (*interpretation*), and shows to others what he or she has seen so that they can see it too (*writing*). Good history begins with respecting people's complexity, not with any kind of preordained certainty. It might well mean using modern techniques that were unknown at the time, such as Freudian psychology or statistical assessment by computer. But good historians always approach the past on its own terms, taking careful stock of the period's cultural norms and people's assumptions or expectations, no matter how different from contemporary attitudes. Even a few decades can offer a surprisingly large gap to bridge, as each generation discovers when it evaluates the accomplishments of those who have come before.

To write history well requires three qualities. One is the courage to try to understand people whom we never can meet — unless our subject is very recent — and to explain events that no one can re-create. The second quality is the humility to realize that we can never entirely appreciate either the people or the events under study. However much evidence is compiled and however smart the questions posed, the past remains too large to contain. It will always continue to surprise.

The third quality historians need is the curiosity that turns sterile facts into clues about a world that once was just as alive, passionate, frightening, and exciting as our own, yet in different ways. Today we know how past events "turned out." But the people taking part had no such knowledge. Good history recaptures those people's fears, hopes, frustrations, failures, and achievements; it tells about people who faced the predicaments and choices that still confront us as we head into the twenty-first century.

All the essays collected in this volume bear on a single, shared problem that the authors agree is important, however differently they may choose to respond to it. On its own, each essay reveals a fine mind coming to grips with a worthwhile question. Taken together, the essays give a sense of just how complex the human situation can be. That point — that human situations are complex — applies just as much to life today as to the lives led in the past. History has no absolute "lessons" to teach; it follows no invariable "laws." But knowing about another time might be of some help as we struggle to live within our own.

EDWARD COUNTRYMAN

Contents

   Dumas Malone

   Herald of Freedom: 1776, From *Jefferson
   the Virginian*

   "So far as form is concerned, the continuing appeal of the
   Declaration lies in the fact that it is clear and simple and that,
   for all its careful craftsmanship and consummate grace, it was
   not so highly polished to lose its edge."

What Did the Declaration Declare?

PART ONE

The Document

The Declaration of Independence

Jefferson's Draft with Revisions

Thomas Jefferson by Rembrandt Peale (1800)

The Declaration of Independence

When in the course of human events, it becomes necessary for one people to dissolve the political bands which have connected them with another, and to assume the Powers of the earth, the separate and equal station to which the Laws of Nature and of Nature's God entitle them, a decent respect to the opinions of mankind requires that they should declare the causes which impel them to the separation.

We hold these truths to be self-evident, that all men are created equal, that they are endowed by their Creator with certain unalienable rights, that among these are Life, Liberty, and the pursuit of Happiness. That to secure these rights, Governments are instituted among Men, deriving their just powers from the consent of the governed. That whenever any Form of Government becomes destructive of these ends, it is the Right of the People to alter or to abolish it, and to institute new Government, laying its foundation on such principles and organizing its powers in such form, as to them shall seem most likely to effect their Safety and Happiness. Prudence, indeed, will dictate that Governments long established should not be changed for light and transient causes; and accordingly all experience hath shown, that mankind are more disposed to suffer, while evils are sufferable, than to right themselves by abolishing the forms to which they are accustomed. But when a long train of abuses and usurpations, pursuing invariably the same Object evinces a design to reduce them under absolute Despotism, it is their right, it is their duty, to throw off such Government, and to provide new Guards for their future security. — Such has been the patient sufferance of these Colonies; and such is now the necessity which constrains them to alter their former Systems of Government. The history of the present King of Great Britain is a history of repeated injuries and usurpations, all having in direct object the establishment of an absolute Tyranny over these States. To prove this, let Facts be submitted to a candid world.

He has refused his Assent to Laws, the most wholesome and necessary for the public good.

He has forbidden his Governors to pass Laws of immediate and pressing importance, unless suspended in their operation till his Assent should be obtained; and when so suspended, he has utterly neglected to attend to them.

He has refused to pass other Laws for the accommodation of large districts of people, unless those people would relinquish the right of Representation in the Legislature, a right inestimable to them and formidable to tyrants only.

He has called together legislative bodies at places unusual, uncomfortable, and distant from the depository of their public Records, for the sole purpose of fatiguing them into compliance with his measures.

He has dissolved Representative Houses repeatedly, for opposing with manly firmness his invasions on the rights of the people.

He has refused for a long time, after such dissolutions, to cause others to be elected; whereby the Legislative powers, incapable of Annihilation, have returned to the People at large for their exercise; the State remaining in the mean time exposed to all dangers of invasion from without, and convulsions within.

He has endeavoured to prevent the population of these States; for that purpose obstructing the Laws of Naturalization of Foreigners; refusing to pass others to encourage their migrations hither, and raising the conditions of new Appropriations of Lands.

He has obstructed the Administration of Justice, by refusing his Assent to Laws for establishing Judiciary powers.

He has made Judges dependent on his Will alone, for the tenure of their offices, and the amount and payment of their salaries.

He has erected a multitude of New Offices, and sent hither swarms of Officers to harass our People, and eat out their substance.

He has kept among us, in times of peace, Standing Armies without the Consent of our legislature.

He has affected to render the Military independent of and superior to the Civil Power.

He has combined with others to subject us to a jurisdiction foreign to our constitution, and unacknowledged by our laws; giving his Assent to their Acts of pretended Legislation.

For quartering large bodies of armed troops among us:

For protecting them, by a mock Trial, from Punishment for any Murders which they should commit on the Inhabitants of these States:

For cutting off our Trade with all parts of the world:

For imposing taxes on us without our Consent:

For depriving us, in many cases, of the benefits of Trial by jury:

For transporting us beyond Seas to be tried for pretended offenses:

For abolishing the free System of English Laws in a neighbouring Province, establishing therein an Arbitrary government, and enlarging its

Boundaries so as to render it at once an example and fit instrument for introducing the same absolute rule into these Colonies:

For taking away our Charters, abolishing our most valuable Laws, and altering fundamentally the Forms of our Governments:

For suspending our own Legislatures, and declaring themselves invested with Power to legislate for us in all cases whatsoever.

He has abdicated Government here, by declaring us out of his Protection and waging War against us.

He has plundered our seas, ravaged our Coasts, burnt our towns, and destroyed the lives of our people.

He is at this time transporting large armies of foreign mercenaries to compleat the works of death, desolation, and tyranny, already begun with circumstances of Cruelty & perfidy scarcely paralleled in the most barbarous ages, and totally unworthy the Head of a civilized nation.

He has constrained our fellow Citizens taken Captive on the high Seas to bear Arms against their Country, to become the executioners of their friends and Brethren, or to fall themselves by their Hands.

He has excited domestic insurrections amongst us, and has endeavoured to bring on the inhabitants of our frontiers, the merciless Indian Savages, whose known rule of warfare, is an undistinguished destruction of all ages, sexes, and conditions.

In every stage of these Oppressions We have Petitioned for Redress in the most humble terms: Our repeated Petitions have been answered only by repeated injury. A Prince, whose character is thus marked by every act which may define a Tyrant, is unfit to be the ruler of a free people.

Nor have We been wanting in attention to our British brethren. We have warned them from time to time of attempts by their legislature to extend an unwarrantable jurisdiction over us. We have reminded them of the circumstances of our emigration and settlement here. We have appealed to their native justice and magnanimity, and we have conjured them by the ties of our common kindred to disavow these usurpations, which, would inevitably interrupt our connections and correspondence. They too must have been deaf to the voice of justice and of consanguinity. We must, therefore, acquiesce in the necessity, which denounces our Separation, and hold them, as we hold the rest of mankind, Enemies in War, in Peace Friends.

WE, THEREFORE, the Representatives of the UNITED STATES OF AMERICA, in General Congress, Assembled, appealing to the Supreme Judge of the world for the rectitude of our intentions, do, in the Name, and by Authority of the good People of these Colonies, solemnly publish and declare, That these United Colonies are, and of Right ought to be FREE AND INDEPENDENT STATES; that they are Absolved from all Allegiance to the British Crown, and that all political connection between them and the State of Great Britain, is and ought to be totally dissolved; and that as Free and Independent States, they have full Power to levy War, conclude Peace, contract Alliances, establish Commerce, and to do all other Acts and Things which Independent States may of right do. And for the support of this Declaration, with a firm reliance on the Protection of Divine Providence, we mutually pledge to each other our Lives, our Fortunes, and our sacred Honor.

The foregoing Declaration was, by order of Congress, engrossed, and signed by the following members:

John Hancock

New Hampshire
Josiah Bartlett
William Whipple
Matthew Thornton

Massachusetts Bay
Samuel Adams
John Adams
Robert Treat Paine
Elbridge Gerry

Rhode Island
Stephen Hopkins
William Ellery

Connecticut
Roger Sherman
Samuel Huntington
William Williams
Oliver Wolcott

New York
William Floyd
Philip Livingston
Francis Lewis
Lewis Morris

New Jersey
Richard Stockton
John Witherspoon
Francis Hopkinson
John Hart
Abraham Clark

Pennsylvania
Robert Morris
Benjamin Rush
Benjamin Franklin
John Morton
George Clymer
James Smith
George Taylor
James Wilson
George Ross

Delaware
Caesar Rodney
George Read
Thomas M'Kean

Maryland
Samuel Chase
William Paca
Thomas Stone
Charles Carroll, of
   Carrollton

Virginia
George Wythe
Richard Henry Lee
Thomas Jefferson
Benjamin Harrison
Thomas Nelson, Jr.
Francis Lightfoot Lee
Carter Braxton

North Carolina
William Hooper
Joseph Hewes
John Penn

South Carolina
Edward Rutledge
Thomas Heyward, Jr.
Thomas Lynch, Jr.
Arthur Middleton

Georgia
Button Gwinnett
Lyman Hall
George Walton

Resolved. That copies of the Declaration be sent to the several assemblies, conventions, and committees, or councils of safety, and to the several commanding officers of the continental troops, that it be proclaimed in each of the United States, at the head of the army.

Jefferson's Draft with Revisions

(Taken from Jefferson's Notes of Proceedings —
Papers, 1:315–19)

I will state the form of the declaration as originally reported. The parts struck out by Congress shall be distinguished by a black line drawn under them; & those inserted by them shall be placed in the margin or in a concurrent column:

A Declaration by the representatives of the United States of America, in [General] Congress assembled

When in the course of human events it becomes necessary for one people to dissolve the political bands which have connected them with another, and to assume among the powers of the earth the separate & equal station to which the laws of nature and of nature's god entitle them, a decent respect to the opinions of mankind requires that they should declare the causes which impel them to the separation.

We hold these truths to be self evident: that all men are created equal; that they are endowed by their creator with
∧ certain   ∧ [inherent and] inalienable rights; that among these are life, liberty & the pursuit of happiness: that to secure these rights, governments are instituted among men, deriving their just powers from the consent of the governed; that whenever any form of government becomes destructive of these ends, it is the right of the people to alter or to abolish it, & to institute new government, laying it's foundation on such principles, & organising it's powers in such form, as to them shall seem most likely to effect their safety & happiness. Prudence indeed will dictate that governments long established should not be changed for light & transient causes; and accordingly all experience hath shewn that mankind are more disposed to suffer while evils are sufferable than to right themselves by

abolishing the forms to which they are accustomed. But when a long train of abuses & usurpations [begun at a distinguished period and] pursuing invariably the same object, evinces a design to reduce them under absolute despotism it is their right, it is their duty to throw off such government, & to provide new guards for their future security. Such has been the patient sufferance of these colonies; & such is now the neces-

∧ alter

sity which constrains them to ∧ [expunge] their former systems of government. The history of the present king of Great

∧ repeated

Britain is a history of ∧ [unremitting] injuries & usurpations, [among which appears no solitary fact to contradict the uni-

∧ all having

form tenor of the rest but all have] ∧ in direct object the establishment of an absolute tyranny over these states. To prove this let facts be submitted to a candid world [for the truth of which we pledge a faith yet unsullied by falsehood.]

He has refused his assent to laws the most wholsome & necessary for the public good.

He has forbidden his governors to pass laws of immediate & pressing importance, unless suspended in their operation till his assent should be obtained; & when so suspended, he has utterly neglected to attend to them.

He has refused to pass other laws for the accommodation of large districts of people, unless those people would relinquish the right of representation in the legislature, a right inestimable to them, & formidable to tyrants only.

He has called together legislative bodies at places unusual, uncomfortable, and distant from the depository of their public records, for the sole purpose of fatiguing them into compliance with his measures.

He has dissolved representative houses repeatedly [& continually] for opposing with manly firmness his invasions on the rights of the people.

He has refused for a long time after such dissolutions to cause others to be elected, whereby the legislative powers, incapable of annihilation, have returned to the people at large for their exercise, the state remaining in the mean time exposed to all the dangers of invasion from without & convulsions within.

He has endeavored to prevent the population of these states; for that purpose obstructing the laws for naturalization of foreigners, refusing to pass others to encourage their migrations hither, & raising the conditions of new appropriations of lands.

∧ obstructed

∧ by

He has ∧ [suffered] the administration of justice [totally to cease in some of these states] ∧ refusing his assent to laws for establishing judiciary powers.

He has made [our] judges dependant on his will alone, for the tenure of their offices, & the amount & paiment of their salaries.

He has erected a multitude of new offices [by a self assumed power] and sent hither swarms of new officers to harrass our people and eat out their substance.

He has kept among us in times of peace standing armies [and ships of war] without the consent of our legislatures.

He has affected to render the military independant of, & superior to the civil power.

He has combined with others to subject us to a jurisdiction foreign to our constitutions & unacknoleged by our laws, giving his assent to their acts of pretended legislation for quartering large bodies of armed troops among us; for protecting them by a mock-trial from punishment for any murders which they should commit on the inhabitants of these states; for cutting off our trade with all parts of the world; for impos-

∧ in many cases

ing taxes on us without our consent; for depriving us ∧ of the benefits of trial by jury; for transporting us beyond seas to be tried for pretended offences; for abolishing the free system of English laws in a neighboring province, establishing therein an arbitrary government, and enlarging it's boundaries, so as to render it at once an example and fit instrument for intro-

∧ colonies

ducing the same absolute rule into these ∧ [states]; for taking away our charters, abolishing our most valuable laws, and altering fundamentally the forms of our governments; for suspending our own legislatures, & declaring themselves invested with power to legislate for us in all cases whatsoever.

∧ by declaring us out of his protection & waging war against us.

He has abdicated government here ∧ [withdrawing his governors, and declaring us out of his allegiance & protection.]

He has plundered our seas, ravaged our coasts, burnt our towns, & destroyed the lives of our people.

∧ scarcely paralleled in the most barbarous ages, & totally

He is at this time transporting large armies of foreign mercenaries to compleat the works of death, desolation & tyranny already begun with circumstances of cruelty and perfidy ∧ unworthy the head of a civilized nation.

He has constrained our fellow citizens taken captive on the high seas to bear arms against their country, to become the executioners of their friends & brethren, or to fall themselves by their hands.

∧ excited
domestic
insurrections
amongst us,
& has

He has ∧ endeavored to bring on the inhabitants of our frontiers and merciless Indian savages, whose known rule of warfare is an undistinguished destruction of all ages, sexes, & conditions [of existence.]

[He has incited treasonable insurrections of our fellow-citizens, with the allurements of forfeiture & confiscation of our property.

He has waged cruel war against human nature itself, violating it's most sacred rights of life and liberty in the persons of a distant people who never offended him, captivating & carrying them into slavery in another hemisphere or to incur miserable death in their transportation thither. This piratical warfare, the opprobrium of *infidel* powers, is the warfare of the *Christian* king of Great Britain. Determined to keep open a market where *Men* should be bought & sold, he has prostituted his negative for suppressing every legislative attempt to prohibit or to restrain·this execrable commerce. And that this assemblage of horrors might want no fact of distinguished die, he is now exciting those very people to rise in arms among us, and to purchase that liberty he has deprived them, by murdering the people on whom he also obtruded them: thus paying off former crimes committed against the *Liberties* of one people, with crimes which he urges them to commit against the *lives* of another.]

In every stage of these oppressions we have petitioned for redress in the most humble terms: our repeated petitions have been answered only by repeated injuries. A prince whose character is thus marked by every act which may define a tyrant is

∧ free

unfit to be the ruler of a ∧ people [who mean to be free. Future ages will scarcely believe that the hardiness of one man adventured, within the short compass of twelve years only, to lay a foundation so broad & so undisguised for tyranny over a people fostered & fixed in principles of freedom.]

Nor have we been wanting in attentions to our British brethren. We have warned them from time to time of attempts

∧ an unwarrantable

∧ us

by their legislature to extend ∧ [a] jurisdiction over ∧ [these our states.] We have reminded them of the circumstances of our emigration & settlement here, [no one of which could warrant so strange a pretension: that these were effected at the expence of our own blood & treasure, unassisted by the wealth or the strength of Great Britain: that in constituting indeed our several forms of government, we had adopted

∧ have

∧ and we have conjured them by

∧ would inevitably

one common king, thereby laying a foundation for perpetual league & amity with them: but that submission to their parliament was no part of our constitution, nor ever in idea, if history may be credited: and,] we ∧ appealed to their native justice and magnanimity ∧ [as well as to] the ties of our common kindred to disavow these usurpations which ∧ [were likely to] interrupt our connection and correspondence. They too have been deaf to the voice of justice & of consanguinity, [and when occasions have been given them, by the regular course of their laws, of removing from their councils the disturbers of our harmony, they have, by their free election, re-established them in power. At this very time too they are permitting their chief magistrate to send over not only souldiers of our common blood, but Scotch & foreign mercenaries to invade & destroy us. These facts have given the last stab to agonizing affection, and manly spirit bids us to

∧ we must therefore

∧ and hold them as we hold the rest of mankind, enemies in war, in peace friends.

renounce for ever these unfeeling brethren. We must endeavor to forget our former love for them, and to hold them as we hold the rest of mankind enemies in war, in peace friends. We might have been a free and a great people together; but a communication of grandeur & of freedom it seems is below their dignity. Be it so, since they will have it. The road to happiness & to glory is open to us too. We will tread it apart from them, and] ∧ acquiesce in the necessity which denounced our [eternal] separation ∧ !

We therefore the representatives of the United states of America in General Congress assembled do in the name, & by the authority of the good people of these [states reject & renounce all allegiance & subjection to the kings of Great Britain & all others who may hereafter claim by, through or under them: we utterly dissolve all political connection which may heretofore have subsisted between us & the people or parliament of Great Britain: & finally we do assert & declare these colonies to be free & independant states,] & that as free & indepen-

We therefore the representatives of the United states of America in General Congress assembled, appealing to the supreme judge of the world for the rectitude of our intentions, do in the name, & by the authority of the good people of these colonies, solemnly publish & declare that these United colonies are & of right ought to be free & independant states; that they are absolved from all allegiance to the British crown, and that all political connection between them & the state of Great Britain is, & ought to be, totally dissolved; & that as free

dant states, they have full power to levy war, conclude peace, contract alliances, establish commerce, & to do all other acts & things which independant states may of right do. And for the support of this declaration we mutually pledge to each other our lives, our fortunes & our sacred honour.

& independant states they have full power to levy war, conclude peace, contract alliances, establish commerce & to do all other acts & things which independant states may of right do.

And for the support of this declaration, with a firm reliance on the protection of divine providence we mutually pledge to each other our lives, our fortunes & our sacred honour.

PART TWO

Introduction

The Enduring Influence of the Declaration

The Enduring Influence
of the Declaration

The Declaration as Mythology and History

Sometime in the middle of June 1776, on the second floor of his temporary lodgings at Seventh and Market Streets in Philadelphia, Thomas Jefferson applied his quill pen to paper on a custom-made portable desk and wrote what have become the magic words of American history. Although historians seldom agree wholeheartedly about anything, there is nearly unanimous consensus that the following fifty-five words constitute the seminal statement of American political culture:

> We hold these truths to be self-evident; that all men are created equal; that they are endowed by their creator with certain inalienable rights; that among these are life, liberty, & the pursuit of happiness; that to secure these rights, governments are instituted among men, deriving their just powers from the consent of the governed.

Although legal scholars who embrace the doctrine of "original intent" are usually referring to the Constitution, it is in fact the Declaration of Independence that captures the essence of America's original promise to itself and the world. Every reform group in American history — from the abolitionists of the 1830s, to the feminists at Seneca Falls in 1848, to the civil rights workers in Mississippi in the 1960s — has harked back to its language and its liberal message. It has served as the inspiration for Abraham Lincoln at Gettysburg in 1863 and for Martin Luther King on the steps of the Lincoln Memorial in 1963. It is the American version of the Magna Carta.

Beyond our national borders, the Declaration has also enjoyed extraordinary influence. Its justification of rebellion against colonial rule has made it a favorite source among indigenous leaders in emerging nations throughout Asia, Africa, and Latin America; even Ho Chi Minh quoted from it when declaring Vietnam free of French imperialism in 1945. The shipyard workers at Gdansk and the protesters in the streets of Prague put its words on the banners they carried to oppose domination by the Soviet Union in the 1980s. And the Chinese students who occupied Tiananmen Square in defiance of communism in 1990 also chanted its language. A compelling case can be made that the Declaration is the best known and most influential political document in both American and world history.

Therein lies an awkward problem for historians. For the Declaration has achieved such mythical potency — has in effect become the core catechism of the American Creed — that any critical appraisal of its origin or meaning seems almost sacrilegious. When, for example, historians raise questions about Jefferson's authorship of the Declaration, or about the different English, Scottish, and French influences on his thinking, or about the elusive meaning of his elegant language, they are inadvertently undermining the sacred character of the Declaration with their profane probings.

For the Declaration is more a creature of mythology than history. In American mythology the gods spoke to Jefferson in that Philadelphia room in June of 1776, and in that miraculous moment the abiding spirit of America became the Word and dwelt amongst us forevermore. Of course, this is an intellectually untenable position that no serious student of American history would defend in public. But it remains the unspoken and unconscious conviction of many American citizens. And the faith on which it rests needs to be noticed at the start as the diamond-hard core of a patriotic mentality that scholars dismiss at their own peril.

The chief problem facing anyone prepared to embrace the mythical version of the Declaration, in addition to the inconvenient fact that supernatural explanations are customarily ruled inadmissible by scholarly judges, is that the magic words mean quite different things to different audiences. In 1861, for example, Lincoln thought the words of the Declaration justified a war against slavery, while leaders of the Confederacy thought the same words justified rebellion against the tyranny of the federal government led by Lincoln. Even today, Americans on both sides of the most controversial questions — affirmative action, abortion, welfare reform — cite the language of the Declaration on behalf of their respective causes and do so, in Carl Becker's immortal phrase, without fear and without research. As a result, the mythologists inadvertently create the impression that the Declaration means whatever one wishes it to mean, which is to say that it means nothing at all.

Clearly, this will not do. Before we can argue cogently about what the Declaration means for us today, we need to know what it meant for Jefferson and his colleagues in the Continental Congress in 1776. Before we celebrate the message of America's political catechism, we need to ask how ordinary Americans understood the message at the time, and by what wholly human means those "present at the creation" made its magic happen. The great text was, in fact, crafted in a specific context. Although conflicting claims about what actually transpired began to surface immediately, to be repeated and inflated in later accounts, the essential facts are known beyond dispute. The story goes like this:

On May 15, 1776, Virginia took the lead by instructing its delegates in the Continental Congress to propose complete American independence from Britain. By then British and American forces had already clashed at Lexington, Concord, and Bunker Hill. For all intents and purposes, the war for independence had started in the spring of 1775, but the formal declaration of American separation from the British Empire had not occurred. Tom Paine's hugely influential pamphlet, *Common Sense,* had appeared in January, 1776, for the first time denouncing not just Parliament's authority but also the legitimacy of monarchy itself. Various state and local committees throughout the thirteen former colonies were busy drafting resolutions and manifestoes in favor of independence (perhaps Jefferson was referring to them when he spoke of "the harmonizing sentiments of the day"). The more moderate members of the Continental Congress still held out hope that the king would come to his senses and offer some conciliatory proposal that might put a halt to the fighting and avert a final break. But such hopes proved illusory. Allegiance to the king was the final obstacle to declaring American independence. It was gradually expiring throughout the spring of 1776.

On June 7, Richard Henry Lee of Virginia moved the resolution "that these United Colonies are, and of right ought to be, free and independent States. . . ." The Congress delayed a vote on Lee's resolution until July 1, in deference to several delegations that were still divided or that needed to confer with their respective colonial legislatures for guidance. In the meantime, the delegates appointed a committee to draft a document implementing Lee's resolution so that, if and when it was approved, the Congress could proceed without pause to publish the decision.

John Adams convened the committee on June 11. It also included Benjamin Franklin, Thomas Jefferson, Robert Livingston, and Roger Sherman. The committee delegated the drafting to Adams and Jefferson, and Adams turned it over to Jefferson. Years later, in his autobiography, Adams recalled that he chose Jefferson because of his reputation as a stylist and also because Adams's own prominence as a leader of the radical faction in the Congress would have subjected the document to greater scrutiny and criticism. Jefferson, according to this account, was more appropriate because he was more innocuous.

Jefferson wrote the first draft of the Declaration of Independence quickly—Adams later claimed it took him only a "day or two"—then showed the draft to Adams and Franklin. They made only a few minor revisions. Then the full committee approved the revised draft and placed the document before the Congress on June 28. After two days of debate, the Congress passed Lee's resolution on July 2. It then began two more days of debate over the wording of the draft of the Declaration. After making several major changes in the text, the Congress approved the final version on July 4 and sent it to the printer for publication. Jefferson later recalled that the Declaration was signed by the members of Congress on that day, but his memory was almost surely incorrect. The parchment copy was not signed by most members until August 2.

Three somewhat sobering insights which defy our mythical sense of the creative moment follow naturally from this version of the story. First, the sense of deep significance we bring to the document did not exist for those who composed, edited, and signed it. They were preoccupied with more pressing military and strategic considerations in the summer of 1776 and did not regard the drafting of the Declaration as their highest priority. Second, Thomas Jefferson was not initially regarded as the author of the Declaration, which was instead considered a collective effort—the work of the entire Congress—rather than the product of one person. Third, that the Declaration articulated a profoundly liberal message about individual freedom and equality was hardly noticed in the revolutionary era. Most contemporaries regarded it as a statement about American political independence from Great Britain, not as America's primal political creed. Only with Lincoln's insistence on the Declaration's creedal implications did the natural rights section of the document move front-and-center as the main claim on America's imagination. Until the middle years of the nineteenth century, in other words, our modern sense of its philosophical significance as the sacred source of American ideals did not exist.

Historians and the Declaration

Although debates about how the Declaration was written and what its words meant began while the participants were still alive, nothing that we would call historical scholarship on the document appeared until the early years of the twentieth century. Not that the Declaration was forgotten or ignored; it soon was trotted out every Fourth of July for celebration in all the towns and villages across the land. But it was so closely tied to the origins of American nationhood, and mythical imperatives that always accompany nation-building cast such a golden haze around the birth of the American republic, that any detached assessment violated the quasi-religious terms of the patriotic faith. (Perhaps the chief value of truths that claimed to be "self-evident," in effect, was that one simply did not need to talk about them.) Unlike the Constitution, which was constantly being brought into the courts and government councils for interpretation and amendment, the Declaration floated above the hurly-burly of political controversy and into a transcendent realm all its own.

The first scholarly study of the context surrounding the Declaration's composition was published in 1906. John H. Hazelton's *The Declaration of Independence: A History* blew away the haze surrounding the Declaration and dispensed with the presumption that its authors were a set of demigods. Hazelton's account established the historical chronology of the drafting process, to include the appointment of the Committee of Five (John Adams, Benjamin Franklin, Thomas Jefferson, Robert Livingston, and Roger Sherman) on June 11, 1776; the decision to make Jefferson the chief draftsman (Franklin was offered the honor, but refused on the grounds that he never wrote anything that would subsequently be edited by a committee); the presentation of the revised draft to the Congress on June 28 (the scene memorialized in the painting by John Trumbull, often mistaken for the signing ceremony); the subsequent debate over the text in the Congress on July 3–4; then the publication of the revised document in Philadelphia on July 4.

Hazelton's ground-breaking detective work was subsequently supplemented by the prodigious research of Julian P. Boyd, whose *The Declaration of Independence: The Evolution of the Text* (1945) filled in gaps in the story, most especially during the crucial weeks between June 11 and June 28 when Jefferson and the Committee of Five were at work. Taken together, Hazelton and Boyd transformed the Declaration from a mystical creation to a man-made historical document. On the basis of their accounts, we know all that we are ever likely to know about the actual composition of the Declaration.

The following facts are now beyond dispute: Jefferson wrote the first draft by himself; the most important influences on his language were his own draft copies of a constitution for Virginia, which he had begun to compose in May, and George Mason's draft for the preamble to the same Virginia Constitution, which contained the felicitous phrase "pursuit of happiness." Jefferson then showed his completed draft to Adams and Franklin, who made only a few changes, the chief one being to insert "self-evident" in lieu of Jefferson's "sacred and undeniable." The full Congress then made eighty-six alterations and excised about one-quarter of Jefferson's text, including one lengthy passage blaming slavery and the slave trade on George III. Despite Boyd's endorsement of Jefferson's claim about a signing ceremony on July 4, there was in all likelihood no single moment when delegates stepped up to sign the Declaration. Jefferson went to his grave believing that every change made by the Congress was a defacement, though the overwhelming scholarly consensus is that the revisions improved the cogency of the final version.

Knowing how and when the words of the Declaration were written provided a solid textual foundation for studying the ideas the words conveyed. The dominant school of thought for the first half of the twentieth century, called the Progressive interpretation, emphasized the rhetorical character of the arguments against the British king and Parliament, describing them as convenient rationalizations that masqueraded as noble ideals. Influenced by the psychological insights of Sigmund Freud and the social assumptions of Karl Marx, the Progressives regarded the political philosophy of the Declaration as mere window dressing or propaganda designed to conceal the economic interests that were actually driving the colonists toward independence.

During the middle decades of the twentieth century the potency of ideas made a historical comeback and a new school of thought, sometimes called the Neo-Whig interpretation, came to dominate the scholarly literature. It saw the Declaration as the logical culmination of a decade-long pamphlet war in which the colonists opposed Parliament's right to tax them or govern their domestic affairs. The Neo-Whigs insisted that the language of the Declaration, along with the earlier pamphlet literature of the preceding decade, should be taken seriously and literally, not just as high-toned propaganda. They tended to emphasize the cogency and sincerity of the arguments against British authority and to trace those arguments back to the Glorious Revolution in England and John Locke's defense of popular sovereignty.

A distinctive variation on the Neo-Whig interpretation has reigned supreme in the last third of the twentieth century. While concurring that we must take the ideas of the Declaration seriously, it extends the understanding of revolutionary ideology beyond traditional notions of political philosophy to encompass the entire range of values, attitudes, and emotions conveyed in the document and its melodramatic or hyperbolic posture toward all forms of political authority. This interpretive school looks back to the English Civil War of the 1640s rather than the Glorious Revolution of 1688 for the roots of opposition thought, and to the radical rather than liberal character of the Declaration's political message, which stigmatizes all political power that is not consensual.

While all three of these interpretive traditions are represented in the following collection of scholarly essays, each selection has been chosen to address a salient question about the Declaration rather than to embody a school of thought. (Unlike fish, historians do not like to travel in schools.) The essay by Dumas Malone is generally regarded as the most elegant and masterful narration of Jefferson's most creative moment. The essay by Carl Becker is the classic account of the Declaration as a liberal and Lockean document. The selection by Garry Wills argues that Becker was wrong and that the major influences on Jefferson's thinking derived from the Scottish rather than English Enlightenment. My own entry acknowledges the influence of various books but sees the Declaration as a projection of Jefferson's highly moralistic and utopian mentality. The final piece by Pauline Maier emphasizes the crucial role of the Continental Congress in editing the Declaration and the collective character of the enterprise.

What all the essays have in common is a historical as opposed to a mythological approach to America's most influential and famous statement of political ideas. They are not intended to constitute the final word on the subject so much as the framework for ongoing inquiry. When it comes to the Declaration of Independence, or for that matter historical scholarship on any significant subject, there can be no end to the argument.

PART THREE

Some Current Questions

The selections that follow deal with some of the issues about the drafting of the Declaration of Independence that now interest historians. Other questions and other selections could have been chosen, but these show the current state of the conversation. Each selection is preceded by a headnote that introduces both its specific subject and its author. After the headnote come Questions for a Closer Reading. The headnote and the questions offer signposts that will allow you to understand more readily what the author is saying. The selections are uncut and they include the original notes. The notes are also signposts for further exploration. If an issue that the author raises intrigues you, use the notes to follow it up. At the end of all the selections are more questions, under the heading Making Connections. Turn to these after you have read the selections, and use them to bring the whole discussion together. In order to answer them, you may find that you need to reread. But no historical source yields up all that is within it to a person content to read it just once.

1. What was Jefferson's role in the drafting of the Declaration?

Dumas Malone

Herald of Freedom: 1776

From *Jefferson the Virginian*

The history of the Declaration of Independence and the biography of Thomas Jefferson intersect in 1776. Dumas Malone was Jefferson's greatest biographer, the author of the magisterial *Jefferson and His Time* (6 volumes), which is generally regarded as the authoritative study of Jefferson's life as well as one of the monuments of modern historical scholarship. The selection reprinted here offers a splendid example of Malone's story-telling skills as well as his ability to combine deep admiration for Jefferson with scrupulous historical accuracy. It focuses on Jefferson's role in the Second Continental Congress in the spring and summer of 1776, when the American movement toward independence was reaching its climax and the Declaration was drafted, revised, and sent out to the world. This is the classic version of one of America's greatest statesmen at his most creative moment. While excellent history, Malone's account also suggests the mythical atmosphere surrounding the Declaration.

Questions for a Closer Reading

1. Why was Jefferson "a natural choice" to draft the Declaration? How does Malone see Jefferson's position on independence develop in the months heading up to June 11?

2. What role did John Adams play and how does Malone feel it was appropriate?

3. Why did the grievance section in the Declaration focus on George III rather than Parliament, which had passed the laws provoking the crisis, or on the *idea* of monarchy?

4. What does Malone say about the underlying philosophy of the Declaration?

5. Why did "Jefferson and some of his Virginia friends" believe that Congress "weakened" the Declaration?

6. How does Jefferson's position as a partisan and participant in the drama, rather than as a historian, color his writing about independence?

7. Malone states that Jefferson's "chief fame from the Declaration lay in the future." Why does our perception of Jefferson's role differ so much today from that of his contemporaries?

Herald of Freedom: 1776

In Virginia, Lord Dunmore ushered in the year 1776 by bombarding Norfolk. Jefferson was on the homeward road by that time but before he left Philadelphia he knew that war had actually begun in his own Province, and, like practically everybody else, he placed the responsibility squarely on the shoulders of the Governor. That dour Scot, after flitting from one ship to another, had issued an emancipation proclamation from

Dumas Malone, *Jefferson the Virginian* (Boston: Little, Brown, 1948), 215–31. Vol. 1 of six-volume biography, *Jefferson and His Time.*

the *William* early in November.[1] It was not destined to rank with Lincoln's. Despite the fact that he retained only the shadow of authority he had declared martial law; and he had summoned the slaves to revolt and join his banner. There was some fighting in the coastal country but he did not have enough troops to make much of a showing. He attracted some runaway slaves and encouraged a few Loyalists, but he served chiefly to infuriate the Virginians and to drive them along the road to independence.

Luckily, Jefferson and his family were remote from the scene of Dunmore's activities, and he reflected that only such places as lay on the water's edge were actually endangered. John Page was much concerned about his house in the Tidewater county of Gloucester, but Monticello was still a haven of peace and the contemporary records of its master reflect little consciousness of a state of war. As county lieutenant he had duties to perform, and it may have been at this time that he carefully listed the volunteers from Albermarle; but he also broached a pipe of Madeira of the vintage of 1770, began to stock his park with deer, and welcomed to his stable another foal of the proud line of Fearnought. For four months he lived as a country gentleman in virtual retirement.[2]

He was quite prepared to resume his public duties as soon as he was really needed, but he welcomed the opportunity to put his thoughts in order and to remain with his wife, about whom he continued to be troubled. He was urged by his friend Nelson, who had his own lady with him in Philadelphia, to bring her with him but she was in no condition to go. It would have been unlike him to give any further explanation, but the chances are that she carried other children than those who finally appeared upon the record and that there were mishaps which went unmentioned.

Jefferson had no special reason to be alarmed about his mother, then living at Shadwell, but on the last day of March she suffered what was supposed to be an apoplectic stroke, lingered for an hour, and died in her fifty-seventh year. He left only a bald and unemotional record of the event, partly through accident it may be, but also because of his consistent reticence in all personal matters.[3] This was just about the date that he had expected to return to Congress, but in the meantime he himself fell ill and was incapacitated for some five weeks longer. The report got around that he was suffering from an inveterate headache which had a hard name; probably it was what we now call migraine. By early May he was over it, and in the fullness of time he descended from the mountain. He would have preferred to go to Williamsburg, where the last and most noted of the Revolutionary conventions of Virginia was assembling, but duty called him to Philadelphia and he was ready.

Accompanied by his servant Bob he went again by the upland route, carrying with him funds he had collected for the purchase of powder for

Virginia and for the relief of the poor in Boston, and after a week's journey he arrived at his old lodgings.[4] Eight days later he removed to a new brick house, three stories high, on the southwest corner of Market and Seventh Streets. This belonged to a bricklayer by the name of Graff (spelled "Graaf" by him), then newly married. Jefferson's quarters on the second floor consisted of a bedroom and parlor, which had the stairs between them. He did his writing in the parlor and commonly used a folding writing-box which his former landlord, the cabinet-maker Benjamin Randolph, had made from Jefferson's own drawing. He still had it half a century later. "It claims no merit of particular beauty," he then said. "It is plain, neat, convenient, and, taking no more room on the writing table than a moderate quarto volume, it yet displays itself sufficiently for any writing." On this box and in this brick house he drafted the Declaration of Independence.[5]

The period of debate was over, as Thomas Paine had said. While Jefferson was still at Monticello he received from Nelson in Philadelphia "a present of 2/ worth of Common Sense," and thus became acquainted with Paine's catalytic pamphlet. Furthermore, he went to great pains to sound out local sentiment before he left home and became convinced that nine tenths of the people in the upper counties favored independence. In Philadelphia he found awaiting him a month-old letter from John Page in which this friend exhorted him: "For God's sake declare the colonies independent and save us from ruin." Also, he had one of the same date from another old college-mate who said: "The notion of independency seems to spread fast in this colony, and will be adopted, I dare say, by a majority of the next convention." But Jefferson was only a delegate to Congress, and he had to await specific instructions from his "country."[6]

On May 15, 1776, the gentlemen in Williamsburg instructed their delegates to propose to Congress that the united colonies be declared free and independent states. Twelve days later these delegates presented their instructions. While the resolution lay on the table in the State House in Philadelphia, the people in Williamsburg generally assumed that Virginia had already declared her independence. Ardent patriots hoisted a new flag, that of the Continental Union, over the Capitol, and the convention proceeded to create a new government. On June 28 it adopted a constitution and there could then be no possible doubt that the Virginians had severed their imperial bonds and embarked on an independent course. Whether the states preceded the Union or the Union preceded the states is as futile a question as that about the hen and the egg, but the historic primacy of the oldest and strongest of the colonies in the cause of freedom was generally and generously recognized. Thus, within a few weeks, this apostrophe appeared in print:

And now, when Britain's mercenary bands
Bombard our cities, desolate our lands,
(Our pray'rs unanswer'd, and our tears in vain,)
While foreign cut-throats crowd th' ensanguin'd plain;
Thy glowing virtue caught the glorious flame,
And first renounc'd the cruel tyrant's name!
With just disdain, and most becoming pride,
Further dependence on the crown deny'd.
Whilst freedom's voice can in these wilds be heard,
Virginia's patriots shall be still rever'd.[7]

During the months of May and June, 1776, one of "Virginia's patriots" was feeling a little sorry for himself in Philadelphia. Jefferson had begun immediately to serve on committees, and these filled up a good deal of time. During this period he dealt particularly with the affairs of Canada, drafting several reports and referring frequently in letters to the misfortunes the American expedition had suffered.[8] He was much more interested in the affairs of Virginia, however, and he made more important use of his new writing-box in drafting a constitution for his own Commonwealth. This document, which he sent to the convention by George Wythe about the middle of June, will be considered later. The main thing to be said here is that Jefferson sent with it a list of charges against King George III, which the convention attached to its new constitution as a preamble. His fellow planters did not follow the precise wording in which he declared the King "deposed," but they did declare that, because of the acts of misrule enumerated by Jefferson, the government of their "country" as formerly exercised under the Crown of Great Britain was totally dissolved. Thus they joined with him in setting the backdrop for a more famous action.

One of his specific recommendations to his own countrymen ought also to be mentioned here. He proposed that such colonies as should be established in Virginia's domain west of the mountains should be "free and independent of this colony and of all the world."[9] He did not intend them to be subordinate. At this early date he advocated the policy which was afterwards embodied in legislative acts of original states and in ordinances of Congress, and which permitted the historic expansion of the American Republic through the creation of new states, equal in all respects to the old. His prophetic finger pointed to the enlarged Union of the future.

In Philadelphia the pace was slower than in Williamsburg, but the tempo was quickening. With customary care the denouncer of George III and the prophet of an expanding confederation made certain notes on proceedings; these he incorporated long years later in his autobiography with a glow of satisfaction.

IN CONGRESS, *Friday, June* 7, 1776. The delegates from Virginia moved in obedience to instructions from their constituents that the Congress should declare that these United colonies are & of right ought to be free & independent states, that they are absolved from all allegiance to the British crown, and that all political connection between them & the state of Great Britain is, & ought to be, totally dissolved; . . .[10]

This was the first of the famous resolutions presented for the delegation by Richard Henry Lee.*

Jefferson did not participate in the debate on the floor that took place a couple of days later, though he noted the arguments. In the course of this debate it appeared to him and others that the middle colonies and South Carolina "were not yet matured for falling from the parent stem, but that they were fast advancing to that state."[11] Accordingly, it was decided to postpone the final decision until July 1, and to appoint a committee in the meantime to prepare a declaration. This consisted of Jefferson, John Adams, Franklin, Roger Sherman, and Robert R. Livingston.[12]

Since Richard Henry Lee had presented the resolution for independence in the first place, there has been much speculation about his failure to be appointed to the committee instead of Jefferson. If this was because of his unpopularity within the Virginia delegation and the desire to build Jefferson up against him, as John Adams said, there was no sign of any alienation of the two men at the time. Two or three days after the committee was named, Lee set out for Virginia to see his ailing wife and to attend the convention in Williamsburg, as apparently he had intended doing all along. There is more reason to suppose that Jefferson envied Lee this opportunity than that Lee envied Jefferson. To both of them the proceedings in Williamsburg seemed more vital at the moment than the drafting of a document in Philadelphia. This particular document they undoubtedly regarded as important, but nobody then knew it would turn out to be immortal. It might not have been if Lee had drawn it.

At all events, it was inevitable that a Virginian should be appointed to the committee and, despite his youth, Jefferson was a natural choice. His voice was uncertain but his pen was known to be potent and there could be no doubt that his mind was prepared. Presumably, the five members met at the house on the Bristol pike where Franklin was confined with the gout, and discussed the general form of the Declaration. Then Jefferson was asked to draft it. Whether or not he and Adams were appointed to a subcommittee, as the latter said and he himself denied, is unimportant; and even if the con-

---

*Richard Henry Lee: Lee (1732–1794) was one of Virginia's most prominent and eloquent statesmen.

versation between the two men did not occur precisely as Adams reported it long afterwards, the reasons which he then assigned were valid. It was the part of wisdom to assign the lead to a Virginian, for the middle colonies were lukewarm and the New Englanders were deliberately keeping themselves in the background at this stage. Also, Jefferson bore no such odium of mistrust and unpopularity as Adams attributed to himself and he was doubtless regarded as the better writer. However, he appears to have submitted his draft first to Adams and then to the ailing Franklin, and an early copy of it in the handwriting of the forthright delegate from Massachusetts survives as a priceless document.[13]

In the seventeen days between June 11, when the committee was appointed, and June 28, when they reported to Congress, Jefferson made his draft. He consulted no book or pamphlet, though he felt entirely free to do so and had no desire to be original. The purposes which he had in mind he afterwards stated with unexcelled frankness and clarity:

> . . . Not to find out new principles, or new arguments, never before thought of, not merely to say things which had never been said before; but to place before mankind the common sense of the subject, in terms so plain and firm as to command their assent, and to justify ourselves in the independent stand we are compelled to take. Neither aiming at originality of principle or sentiment, nor yet copied from any particular and previous writing, it was intended to be an expression of the American mind, and to give to that expression the proper tone and spirit called for by the occasion.[14]

He did copy a good deal from a particular and previous writing of his own. Besides his writing-box he spread out the charges against the King which he had sent to Virginia. These constituted the substantial foundation of the longest section in the Declaration. Another paper, which his fellow Virginians adopted before their constitution, was also available to him: the Declaration of Rights, largely drafted by George Mason and afterwards renowned. The phraseology of the even more famous philosophical paragraph in the intercolonial Declaration is similar to parts of this and may reflect its direct influence. Jefferson could have drawn on George Mason for his own statement of fundamental human rights, and he would have thought this not amiss, but the ideas were in his mind already. They belonged to no single man but, in his opinion, were the property of mankind. Certainly they were the property of the American Patriots, whose mind he was trying to express, and it really made no difference where they came from.

Jefferson's task was to impart the proper tone and spirit, and to do this he labored long. He was a ready writer but he could also be a fastidious one, and he never weighed his phrases more carefully than now. He even corrected the paper after it was formally adopted, in order to get a better word. He regarded capitalization and spelling with considerable indifference in letters, but here he went to unusual pains to regularize them.

The history of the evolving text of the Declaration has been studied by scholars with great care, in the effort to determine the authorship of every phrase and to distribute credit with impartial hand. Certain minor changes can be credited to Adams and Franklin; the authorship of others which Jefferson inserted at a later time in his Rough Draft will probably remain forever doubtful. In the first place he wrote: "We hold these truths to be sacred and undeniable." We cannot be sure whether it was he or Franklin who substituted "self-evident."[15] It is possible that the expression "unalienable rights" was owing to a printer's error, for Jefferson himself wrote "inalienable." The changes have been counted and recounted, but the ones made by his colleagues on the committee appear to have been few, and the document they approved and reported on June 28 was undeniably Jefferson's. Then it ran the gamut of Congress — to his own deep chagrin but with results that were generally beneficial.

Congress properly kept it on the table for a few days, for they still had to reach a decision on the question of independence itself. It was on July 2 that this question, which John Adams described as the greatest that ever was debated in America, was decided.[16] The resolution originally presented by Richard Henry Lee was then adopted and the delegates as a group were free to consider the precise form of the Declaration. They examined it during the three days, July 2–4. Jefferson dutifully observed the proprieties by listening in silence while less partial judges commented on the merits and demerits of his work. John Adams loyally supported every word of it, however, and Benjamin Franklin told him a comforting story while he writhed. This was about a hatter, whose inscription for a handsome signboard was subjected to such criticism that it was finally reduced to his name and the figure of a hat.[17]

Jefferson and some of his Virginia friends believed that Congress weakened the Declaration, but there can now be little doubt that the critics strengthened it. This they did primarily by deletion. The most important single omission was the perfervid charge against the King about the slave trade. In simpler form this had been accepted by Jefferson's fellow Virginians, who had included it in the preamble to their constitution just as he wrote it, even though they did not then outlaw the slave trade as he desired. In Congress, the South Carolinians and Georgians favored the continuance of the traffic; and certain of the Northern brethren were dubious about such sweeping condemnation, being aware that some of their people had engaged in the dirty business. Others besides George III were blameable. From the literary point of view this omission was no loss, for the charge was really out of character with the rest of the document. It was one of those rare Jeffersonian passages which are consciously rhetorical and betray a striving for effect.[18]

Also, Congress rewrote and greatly reduced the final paragraph, attaching to it, not Jefferson's assertion of independence, but the original resolution of Lee. These changes contributed to directness and thus constituted an improvement, but from Jefferson's Rough Draft certain touching expressions may be resurrected and allowed to speak for themselves — such, for example, as these: "We must endeavor to forget our former love for them, . . . We might have been a free and a great people together; . . ." Plenty of felicitous phrases were left — more, probably, than in any other of Jefferson's compositions and quite enough for any single document. In the last sentence Congress inserted the phrase, "with a firm reliance on the protection of divine providence," but left his final words in their original form except for capitalization: "we mutually pledge to each other our lives, our Fortunes, and our sacred Honour." They could not improve on these.

The literary excellence of the Declaration is best attested by the fact that it has stood the test of time. It became the most popular state paper of the American Republic not merely because it was the first, but also because to most people it has seemed the best. No other American document has been read so often or listened to by so many weary and perspiring audiences. Yet, despite interminable repetition, those well-worn phrases have never lost their potency and charm.[19] So far as form is concerned, the continuing appeal of the Declaration lies in the fact that it is clear and simple and that, for all its careful craftsmanship and consummate grace, it was not so highly polished as to lose its edge. Only in its reiterated charges against the King does it even approach the declamatory. It may lack the stark grandeur of certain passages from Lincoln, it may be almost too felicitous; but it has notable elevation of spirit and solemnity of tone. Intended as an expression of the American mind, it was also Jefferson at his literary best.[20]

Its immediate purpose was to justify the secession of the colonies from the Mother Country. Thus, as every American should know, the great document begins:

> When in the Course of human events, it becomes necessary for one people to dissolve the political bands, which have connected them with another, and to assume among the powers of the earth, the separate and equal station to which the Laws of Nature and of Nature's God entitle them, a decent respect to the opinions of mankind requires that they should declare the causes which impel them to the separation.

It is hard to see how Jefferson could have combined in such compass a larger number of important ideas or could have better imparted the tone of dignity, solemnity, respectful firmness, and injured virtue which the circumstances required. It was *necessary* to dissolve these old political bands. The American people were *entitled* to an independent station under the laws of God and Nature, but they had a *decent respect* to the opinions of mankind and were thus impelled to give reasons for their course.

Before stating the specific reasons he took the whole controversy out of the realm of petty and selfish squabbling by setting it on a high background of philosophy. The philosophical passage in the Declaration, which he wrote as a single brief paragraph, became the most famous part of the document; and, as a summary of human rights and a justification of revolution in behalf of them, it is doubtful if it has ever been excelled. Actually he outlined a whole system of philosophy in a few sentences.[21] To this epitome of current wisdom, which he himself regarded as a creed, we must turn again as men have done through the generations. At the time, however, attention was focused on the specific rather than on the general grounds of revolution, for these were familiar to others besides enlightened gentlemen and the statement of them awakened echoes in more minds.

The charges in the Declaration were directed, not against the British people or the British Parliament, but against the King. There was definite purpose in this. Jefferson, and the great body of the Patriots with him, had already repudiated the authority of Parliament, and in his *Summary View** he had made a futile appeal to the Monarch. Now, this last tie was to be cut and the onus must be put on George III himself. Such a personification of grievances was unwarranted on strict historical grounds. This was the language of political controversy, not that of dispassionate scholarship. Nevertheless, in these charges Jefferson gave an extraordinarily full summary of the whole controversy with the Mother Country. He included the major grievances against Parliament by a clever literary device which avoided even the mention of that name.

> . . . He [the King] has combined with others to subject us to a jurisdiction foreign to our constitution, and unacknowledged by our laws; giving his Assent to their Acts of pretended Legislation.

Certain acts of "pretended" legislation were then specified.

At the bar of history these charges now seem extreme. Almost any modern historian can make a better case for the British authorities than Jefferson did, for he really granted them no case at all. This is not to say that he made any charge which could not have been backed by facts. These griev-

---

* *Summary View:* Jefferson's *A Summary View of the Rights of British America,* which appeared in 1774, had focused its argument against the authority of Parliament over the American colonies.

ances were actual not imaginary; they recalled in every instance specific policies and events. The constituted a "long train of abuses" and certain of them could properly be termed "usurpations," but historians of a later generation, who have been in position to study this controversy calmly, assign most of them to official stupidity or to helplessness in the face of the larger imperial problem, rather than to a deliberate design to reduce the colonies "under absolute despotism." By implication, certain of these charges were manifestly unjust. The causes of the American Revolution cannot be adduced from the Declaration alone, and Jefferson may be charged with over-simplifying an exceedingly complicated situation. This would have been a fault in an historian but under the circumstances it may be regarded as a virtue in a statesman.

He carried this over-simplification even further in another paper, which was written five years later and has remained obscure. In an address to an Indian chief, toward the end of his governorship of Virginia, he described the causes of the Revolution as a teacher might to a child.

> . . . You find us, brother, engaged in war with a powerful nation. Our forefathers were Englishmen, inhabitants of a little island beyond the great water, and, being distressed for land, they came and settled here. As long as we were young and weak, the English whom we had left behind, made us carry all our wealth to their country, to enrich them; and, not satisfied with this, they at length began to say we were their slaves, and should do whatever they ordered us. We were now grown up and felt ourselves strong; we knew we were free as they were, that we came here of our own accord and not at their biddance, and were determined to be free as long as we should exist. For this reason they made war on us.[22]

This sounds much *too* simple. But Jefferson's failure to allow for the complexities of the imperial problem and to grant any credit to British good will cannot be attributed to the fact that he had a simple mind or conspicuously lacked a sense of historical justice. The relativity of circumstances must always be remembered. On the verge of revolution Jefferson and his colleagues could not be expected to be dispassionate; he had long since weighed the conflicting arguments, and the preponderance on the Patriots' side seemed so great that he saw no need for apothecary's scales. He was wandering in no mist of doubt, seeking the totality of truth. His task as a statesman was to grasp the essence of the controversy, and as the penman of independence to set it forth — not in neutral shades but in bold contrasts of black and white.

To his mind the fundamental issue was simple: British policy constituted a perilous threat to liberties that were dearer to him than life itself. Furthermore, he was convinced that British policy centered in the personality and was inseparable from the determination of a stubborn King. To him George III was not merely a symbol but a powerful personal obstacle to the sort of self-government he and his fellows were claiming as a natural human right. In his own mind he coupled the monarch with ill-fated Charles I. That year Jefferson heard from Benjamin Franklin a motto which he attributed to one of the regicides: "Rebellion to tyrants is obedience to God." He seized upon this immediately, put it on his own seal later, and made it a personal slogan throughout life.[23] In 1776 especially this was a stirring call to action, for the historical circumstances seemed to him strikingly analogous to those that had led to the successful revolt against the Stuart King. Jefferson was not a complete historian; and if a philosopher is one who can never quite make up his mind, he was no philosopher. If passionate devotion to causes one deems fundamental is partisanship, he was very generally a partisan, and certainly was one at this stage. But at no time afterwards did he ever doubt that his general estimate of this situation was correct.

He did not change his opinion about George III when he met him ten years later; but, considering the Declaration toward the end of his own life, he himself valued the "principles of the instrument" more than his wholesale indictment of British policy at the age of thirty-three.[24] Such, also, has been the judgment of history. It is not for the charges against the King but for the brief philosophical paragraph that posterity has been most grateful to him. Said Abraham Lincoln when the author of the Declaration had been dead for a generation: "All honor to Jefferson — to the man, who in the concrete pressure of a struggle for national independence by a single people, had the coolness, forecaste [sic], and sagacity to introduce into a merely revolutionary document an abstract truth, applicable to all men and all times, and so to embalm it there that to-day and in all coming days it shall be a rebuke and a stumbling-block to the very harbingers of reappearing tyranny and oppression."[25] These words from Lincoln could have been echoed with eminent appropriateness during the latest and greatest of wars, for the doctrines of the Declaration stand in complete antithesis to those which the totalitarians of the twentieth century proclaimed. Jefferson's words should make tyranny tremble in any age.

They have alarmed conservative minds in his own land in every generation, and some compatriots of his have regretted that the new Republic was dedicated to such radical doctrines at its birth. Whether it would have been thus dedicated, amid such incense of universalism, if Jefferson had not officiated at the altar, no man can say. At the dawn of American independence Congress made his words official and held "these truths to be self-evident; that all men are created equal; that they are endowed by their Creator with certain unalienable rights; that among these are life, liberty, and the pursuit of happiness; that to secure these rights, governments are instituted among men, deriving their just powers from the consent of the governed."

The immediate deduction was the right of revolution against a government which was destructive of these ends. Another deduction was inescapable: the governments to be established here must aim first of all to secure these rights. American democracy might have developed as the resultant of other forces, geographical and economic, but the fact is that this passage became its major charter. "The history of American democracy," as has been wisely said, "is a gradual realization, too slow for some and too rapid for others, of the implications of the Declaration of Independence."[26]

It will require a long book to show in convincing detail what Jefferson himself sought to realize, how he tried to do it, how he both succeeded and failed; but two important questions of implication should be raised here. One is about property, which he did not mention in this famous passage; the other is about the natural equality of men, which he proclaimed.

Was there any significance in his omission of the word "property," which had been used by John Locke, and his substitution for it of the phrase "pursuit of happiness"? It is exceedingly doubtful that his contemporaries thought there was. Locke presupposed the pursuit of happiness, and Jefferson always assumed as basic the right of an individual to hold property. He did not anticipate communism. Nevertheless, his use here of a more inclusive phrase than the word "property" was probably deliberate, and if it does not clearly indicate a philosophical distinction between different sorts of rights it does suggest the characteristic shading of his thought. From his later statements and actions there can be no doubt that such rights as freedom of mind, conscience, and person were the ones he cherished most. These unquestionably were inalienable, and also desirable in themselves; property was indispensable, just as government was, but, like it, was a means to human happiness and not an end.[27]

Other expressions then seemed much more significant. At the Virginia convention shortly before this, during the discussion of George Mason's Declaration of Rights, certain "aristocrats" objected to the statement that men are by nature equally free and independent, "as being the forerunner or pretext of civil convulsion." The revolutionary character of the doctrine was recognized. The objectors were calmed down, however, by the observation that this was mostly talk and that the generalization did not apply to slaves, at any rate.[28] If Jefferson had been present and had been questioned on this point he would have said that the general statement did apply to slaves, and that these unfortunate creatures had lost their freedom and all semblance of equality through the operation of human law, which in this respect was in conflict with the higher law of Nature. His own recommendations to that convention do not reveal him as an impatient reformer, and in reality he never became one, but they leave no doubt that he took his own philosophy seriously. Slavery in his native region was one of the contradictions he always had to face; it was one of the tyrannical forms he was unable to abolish. The natural equality he talked about was not that of intellectual endowment, but, as Lincoln so clearly perceived, he proclaimed for all time the dignity of human nature.

At a crucial moment in 1776, Congress was under the control of men who were willing to adopt, under the pressure of imperial circumstances, what amounted to a charter of individual liberty and human rights, and to inscribe it indelibly on the page of history. This was translated into democratic terms as soon as men began to employ them widely. Thus a sensitive and fastidious gentleman, who prized privacy and disliked the rabble, became a major prophet not only of freedom but also of democracy. He himself was slower to use the latter term than to realize the implications of his doctrine, and his actions at this time were not motivated by personal political ambition. Nor had he proceeded in a mood of sentimentality. He felt with his mind and his mind left him in no doubt that what he had said was right.

On July 4 this thoughtful and observant man arose at dawn according to his custom, noting in the back of his Account Book that the temperature was 68° Fahrenheit at 6 A.M. On his way to or from the State House that very day he paid for a thermometer, but undoubtedly he had used this or another one already. His record of the temperature from this time forward, wherever he happened to be, was practically unbroken. He never ceased being interested in climate, though he believed that likes and dislikes in this respect were largely a matter of habit. To one of his upbringing this day must have been quite comfortable. His highest reading of the thermometer, 76°, was at one o'clock. His thoughts were not wholly of the place and season, however, for on that day he also paid for seven pairs of women's gloves, destined for Monticello.

On July 4, 1776, at Oxford, where Lord North was chancellor, honorary degrees were conferred by that ancient and honorable university on Thomas Hutchinson, late Governor of Massachusetts Bay, and Peter Oliver, late Deputy Governor.[29] In England they could not be expected to know just what was happening in Congress, and not even the delegates in Philadelphia thought of this as the birthday of the American Republic.

The great decision was made on July 2, when the resolution of independence was adopted. What actually happened on July 4 was that twelve states agreed to the written Declaration embodying this resolution, while the delegates from New York refrained from voting. The action did not become unanimous until July 15, when the resolutions of the New York convention were laid before Congress. In the meantime, the Declaration was authenticated by the bold signature of President John Hancock, and by that of Secretary Charles Thomson; it was printed and transmitted to the various assemblies, conventions, committees, and commanding officers; and on July 8 in Philadelphia it was first proclaimed by the local Committee of Safety. John Adams has left a brief account of this event, which occurred in the State House yard in the presence of a great crowd of people.[30]

Jefferson must have been present but he was not in the spotlight; nobody announced that he was the author of this paper or led him forward upon the stage to take a bow. Cheers mounted to the sky; battalions paraded on the Common; and the bells rang all day and most of the night. This was in celebration not of a document but of an event. The tie with the Mother Country had been cut and Congress as a body was responsible for that dangerous and fateful action. Not until July 19 did Congress order that the Declaration be engrossed on parchment and signed by the members. Jefferson himself could not have affixed his own name until August 2. The names of the delegates were well known, but the signatures themselves were not made public until the following January and Jefferson's was one of many, even then.

This is another way of saying that his chief fame from the Declaration lay in the future. As he poked around the shops of Philadelphia bystanders may have pointed him out as an influential delegate, but they did not hail him as the author and he probably would not have wanted them to. At the moment, in fact, his pride in authorship was slight, for he believed that Congress had manhandled his composition and marred its strength. He cared little for general applause but he wanted to guard his own literary reputation among the select. He made copies of his own draft as it had emerged from the committee, and sent these to some of his friends; they could compare it with the final version and judge whether it was better or worse for the critics.[31]

Richard Henry Lee, who was entitled to a copy on other grounds, believed that the critics had "mangled" the paper, and most of Jefferson's friends in Virginia sent comments which were gratifying to him personally. Pendleton thought the charges against the King an improvement over those in the preamble to the Virginia constitution, and John Page was highly pleased with the Declaration as a whole. But these friends did not differentiate sharply between the act of asserting independence and the document in the case. Thus Lee said that the "Thing itself"— that is, independence —was so good that no cookery could spoil the dish for the palates of freemen. Nobody regarded the paper as in any sense a private affair and Page's prayer was the natural and proper one: "God preserve the United States."[32]

Nobody except Jefferson himself took his wounded pride as an author very seriously and he proceeded to dismiss the paper from his mind. He kept his contemporary record of events, but not until later did he put them in their present form and by that time his memory was confused. Because of an ambiguous statement in what passed for the official record, he, like nearly everybody else, forgot the exact date at which he affixed his signature. As an old man he talked much about such antiquarian matters, because they were so often referred to him, but in July, 1776, the most important fact was that independence had been proclaimed in the name of the officers of the Continental Congress. This was political revolution and it brought grave dangers in its train. Jefferson did not forget, however, that in a moment of high faith he had formulated a creed for himself and the Republic. His dominant concern henceforth was to translate this into legal institutions and to make it a living reality. During the next three years in Virginia he devoted himself more impressively to this task than to the more immediate one of winning the war and the equally imperative one of establishing a more perfect Union.

Notes

1. Nov. 7, 1775. See *Dunmore's Proclamation of Emancipation,* with an account by Francis Berkeley (McGregor Library, Univ. of Va., 1941).

2. Page to Jefferson, Nov. 11, [1775], Library of Congress [LC], 2:178–81; list of volunteers, LC, 6:1063; Account Book, Jan. 28, Feb. 8, Mar. 26, 1776.

3. Account Book, Mar. 31, 1776; Jefferson to — Randolph, Aug.–Sept. 1776, Massachusetts Historical Society [MHS], University of Virginia photostat. [Jefferson's informal account books are in various repositories. — Ed.]

4. Details in Account Book, beginning May 7, 1776.

5. On the box, see his letter to Ellen Coolidge, Nov. 14, 1825, Jefferson Papers, Collections of the Massachusetts Historical Society, 7 ser., I, p. 361; on the house, the thoroughly documented account in J. H. Hazelton, *Declaration of Independence* (1906), pp. 149–54.

6. From Thomas Nelson, Jr., Feb. 4, 1776, *New-England Historical & Genealogical Register,* LVI, 54; from Page, Apr. 6, 1776, Ibid., LVI, 55; from James McClurg, Apr. 6, 1776, LC, 2:216; to Nelson, May 16, 1776, Ford, II, 3.

7. July 27, 1776; Frank Moore, *Diary of the Revolution* (1876), quoting *Freeman's Journal.*

8. See particularly reports of May 21, June 17, 1776 (Paul Leicester Ford, ed., *The Writings of Thomas Jefferson* (New York and London, 1899), II, 4–6, 30–39); letters to Nelson, May 19, to Fleming, July 1, and to Eppes, July 15 Ibid., II, 3, 39–40, 53–64).

9. Ford, 11, 26.

10. Ford, I, 18. Other resolutions related to foreign alliances and a confederation.

11. Ibid., 24; see also 19–24.

12. June 11, 1776, *Journals of the Continental Congress* (34 vols., Washington, D.C., 1904–36), V, 429.

13. See the admirable study of J. P. Boyd, *The Declaration of Independence;* pp. 9–12, 40, Document IV, etc. Later discoveries are incorporated in an article by the same editor in the *New York Times,* Apr. 13, 1947. These include a letter from Franklin to Benj. Rush, June 26, 1776, discovered by Lyman H. Butterfield, implying that Franklin was confined to the house of Edward Duffield on the Bristol Pike, during June. The partially conflicting accounts of Jefferson and Adams are in Ford, I, 24–27 n., and J. H. Hazelton, *Declaration of Independence,* pp. 141–46. See also Carl Becker's brilliant work, *The Declaration of Independence,* ch. IV.

14. To Henry Lee, May 8, 1825; Ford, X, 343.

15. Boyd, p. 22; Document V, p. 1. Since the discovery of a still earlier draft, he thinks the "Rough Draft" should really be called the "Committee Draft."

16. To Mrs. Adams, July 3, 1776; John Adams, *Works,* ed. C. F. Adams [*Works*] (10 vols., Boston, 1856), IX, 418.

17. Ford, X, 119–20 n., 268.

18. Becker, *Declaration of Independence,* pp. 212–16.

19. See M. C. Tyler, in *Literary History of the American Revolution* (1897), I, 520–21.

20. The best discussion of the literary qualities I know of is that of Carl Becker, *Declaration of Independence,* ch. 5.

21. Well summarized in R. B. Perry, *Puritanism and Democracy,* p. 125.

22. Address to Brother John Baptist de Coigne, June 1781 (*Writings of Thomas Jefferson,* ed. A. A. Lipscomb and A. E. Bergh [L. & B.], XVI, 372).

23. Franklin suggested the motto for the seal of the United States in the summer of 1776; see references to this and to Jefferson's own seal in the following chapter. For Jefferson's crediting the motto to a regicide, see his letter to Edward Everett, Feb. 24, 1823 (L. & B., XV, 415).

24. To Madison, Aug. 30, 1823; Ford, X, 269.

25. Apr. 6, 1859, to H. L. Pierce and others, responding to an invitation to attend a celebration in honor of Jefferson's birthday in Boston (L. & B., I, xvii).

26. Ralph Barton Perry, in *Puritanism and Democracy,* p. 133.

27. This question is ably summarized and discussed by Perry, Ibid., pp. 184–86, with citations. Gilbert Chinard holds to the position that Jefferson made a definite distinction between inalienable rights and rights of a second class, though he sees in him no hostility to property; *Thomas Jefferson* (2nd ed., revised, 1939), pp. 80–85. Adrienne Koch finds ample proof for Jefferson's recognition of the right to property as a basic natural right; *Philosophy of Thomas Jefferson,* p. 175. The claim made by Parrington that Jefferson's action marked a complete breach with the Whiggish doctrine of property rights is extreme; *Main Currents in American Thought,* I, 344. A good statement of Jefferson's later attitude toward different sorts of rights is in his letter to Noah Webster, Dec. 4, 1790, in Ford, V, 254–55.

28. Robert Leroy Hilldrup, *Life and Times of Edmund Pendleton* (Chapel Hill, 1939), pp. 169–70, citing Kate Mason Rowland, *The Life of George Mason, 1725–1792, Including his Speeches, Public Papers, and Correspondence* (2 vols., London, 1888), I, 240. The original authority for the observation, however, is Edmund Randolph; see *Virginia Magazine,* XLIV, 45. The inapplicability of the Declaration of Rights to slaves and free Negroes was affirmed by the Virginia courts at a later time, in disagreement with Jefferson's friend George Wythe; Margaret V. Nelson, *A Study of Judicial Review in Virginia, 1789–1928* (New York, 1947), p. 184.

29. *Annual Register, 1776* (4 ed., London, 1788), p. 159.

30. To Samuel Chase, July 9, 1776; *Works,* IX, 420. For an admirable summary of chronology, see Adams, *Letters of Members of the Continental Congress,* ed., E. C. Burnett, pp. 188–97.

31. To R. H. Lee, July 8, 1776; Ford, II, 259. In *The Declaration of Independence,* Boyd reproduces all the known drafts and copies in Jefferson's hand. These include the copies made for Lee and Wythe and an unidentified copy which may have been sent to Pendleton or John Page.

32. To William Fleming, July 1, 1776, Ford, II, 41; from R. H. Lee, July 21, 1776, Richard Henry Lee, *Letters,* ed. J. C. Ballagh (2 vols., New York, Macmillan, 1911, 1914), I, 210; from Page, July 20, 1776 (*N.-Eng. Hist. & Genealog. Reg.,* LVI, 152); from Pendleton, July 22, 1776 (LC, II, 277). For general comments on contemporary indifference to the Declaration as a document, see J. C. Fitzpatrick, *Spirit of the Revolution,* esp. ch. 2.

2. Is the philosophy of the Declaration Lockean?

Carl Becker

The Natural Rights Philosophy

From *The Declaration of Independence:
A Study in the History of Political Ideas*

No one has had a greater influence on how historians think about the Declaration of Independence than Carl Becker. In a deceptively simple style, fully as felicitous as Jefferson's, Becker described the Declaration as Jefferson's meditation on John Locke. Unlike Malone, who was most interested in the political narrative surrounding the drafting process and beyond, Becker was concerned with the intellectual legacy Jefferson drew upon for his ideas. He located that legacy in the English and French Enlightenment and the core of Jefferson's inspiration in Locke's *Second Treatise on Government.* The story Becker told made the Lockean interpretation of the Declaration seem as self-evident as Jefferson's famous truths. Along the way, somewhat mischievously, Becker, a historian of the Progressive school, implied that the ideas Jefferson announced were rationalizations for the unspoken interests of the colonists and therefore mere afterthoughts for actions already decided upon before the summer of '76.

Questions for a Closer Reading

1. How does Becker explain Jefferson's affinity for the ideas articulated by Locke?

2. Why does Becker devote so much space to European books and thinkers not directly connected to the political story of America in 1776?

3. What are the implications for the Declaration of realizing how Locke influenced Jefferson?

4. In what sense is Becker's version of the ideas underlying the Declaration subversive? How does Becker's suggestion that the Declaration rationalized the colonial revolt after the fact alter our perception of the document?

5. How does the extended philosophical heritage of the Declaration set forth in this selection help us understand the important phrase, "life, liberty, and the pursuit of happiness"?

The Natural Rights Philosophy

Whether the political philosophy of the Declaration of Independence is "true" or "false" has been much discussed. In the late eighteenth century it was widely accepted as a commonplace. At a later time, in 1822, John Adams made this a ground for detracting from the significance of Jefferson's share in the authorship of the famous document. He was perhaps a little irritated by the laudation which Fourth of July orators were lavishing on his friend, and wished to remind his countrymen that others had had a hand in the affair. "There is not an idea in it," he wrote to Pickering, "but what had been hackneyed in Congress for two years before."[1] This is substantially true; but as a criticism, if it was intended as such, it is wholly irrelevant, since the strength of the Declaration was precisely that it said what everyone was thinking. Nothing could have been more futile than an attempt to justify a revolution on principles which no one had ever heard of before.

In replying to Adams' strictures, Jefferson had only to state this simple fact.

Pickering's observations, and Mr. Adams' in addition, that it contained no new ideas, that it is a commonplace compilation, its sentiments hacknied in

Carl Becker, *The Declaration of Independence: A Study in the History of Political Ideas* (New York, 1922; reprinted 1942; Vintage, 1958), 24–41, 51–79.

Congress for two years before . . . may all be true. Of that I am not to be the judge. Richard H. Lee charged it as copied from Locke's treatise on Government. . . . I know only that I turned to neither book nor pamphlet while writing it. I did not consider it as any part of my charge to invent new ideas altogether and to offer no sentiment which had ever been expressed before.[2]

In writing to Lee, in 1825, Jefferson said again that he only attempted to express the ideas of the Whigs, who all thought alike on the subject. The essential thing was

> Not to find out new principles, or new arguments, never before thought of, not merely to say things which had never been said before; but to place before mankind the common sense of the subject, in terms so plain and firm as to command their assent. . . . Neither aiming at originality of principles or sentiments, nor yet copied from any particular and previous writing, it was intended to be an expression of the American mind. . . . All its authority rests then on the harmonizing sentiments of the day, whether expressed in conversation, in letters, printed essays, or the elementary books of public right, as Aristotle, Cicero, Locke, Sidney, etc.[3]

Not all Americans, it is true, would have accepted the philosophy of the Declaration, just as Jefferson phrased it, without qualification, as the "common sense of the subject"; but one may say that the premises of this philosophy, the underlying preconceptions from which it is derived, were commonly taken for granted. That there is a 'natural order' of things in the world, cleverly and expertly designed by God for the guidance of mankind; that the 'laws' of this natural order may be discovered by human reason; that these laws so discovered furnish a reliable and immutable standard for testing the ideas, the conduct, and the institutions of men — these were the accepted premises, the preconceptions, of most eighteenth-century thinking, not only in America but also in England and France. They were, as Jefferson says, the "sentiments of the day, whether expressed in conversation, in letters, printed essays, or the elementary books of public right." Where Jefferson got his ideas is hardly so much a question as where he could have got away from them.

Since these sentiments of the day were common in France, and were most copiously, and perhaps most logically, expressed there, it has sometimes been thought that Jefferson and his American contemporaries must have borrowed their ideas from French writers, must have been "influenced" by them, for example by Rousseau. But it does not appear that Jefferson, or any American, read many French books. So far as the "Fathers" were, before 1776, directly influenced by particular writers, the writers were English, and notably Locke. Most Americans had absorbed Locke's works as a kind of political gospel; and the Declaration, in its form, in its phraseology, follows closely certain sentences in Locke's second treatise on government. This is interesting, but it does not tell us why Jefferson, having read Locke's treatise, was so taken with it that he read it again, and still again, so that afterwards its very phrases reappear in his own writing. Jefferson doubtless read Filmer * as well as Locke; but the phrases of Filmer, happily, do not appear in the Declaration. Generally speaking, men are influenced by books which clarify their own thought, which express their own notions well, or which suggest to them ideas which their minds are already predisposed to accept. If Jefferson had read Rousseau's *Social Contract* we may be sure he would have been strongly impressed by it. What has to be explained is why the best minds of the eighteenth century were so ready to be impressed by Locke's treatise on civil government and by Rousseau's *Social Contract*. What we have to seek is the origin of those common underlying preconceptions that made the minds of many men, in different countries, run along the same track in their political thinking.

It is well known that Locke's treatise, written in reply to Filmer's *Patriarcha*, was an apology for the Revolution of 1688. "Kings," said Filmer, "are as absolute as Adam over the creatures"; and in general the Stuart partisans had taken their stand, as Sir Frederick Pollock says, "on a supposed indefeasible right of kings, derived from a supposed divine institution of monarchy. ... The Whigs needed an antidote, and Locke found one in his modified version of the original compact."[4] This means that political circumstances had brought the Whigs to the point of overturning the existing government, that they were human enough to wish to feel that this was a decent and right thing to do, and that, accordingly, their minds were disposed to welcome a reasoned theory of politics which would make their revolution, as a particular example under the general rule, respectable and meritorious. The Whigs needed a theory of politics that would make their revolution of 1688 a "glorious revolution." Locke said himself that he had made all his discoveries by "steadily intending his mind in a given direction." Inevitably the Whigs steadily "intended their minds" away from the idea of a divine right in kings, since no glorious revolution was to be found there, and towards a new idea — in fact, towards Locke's modified version of the compact theory.

It is significant that English writers were formulating a new version of the compact theory in the seventeenth century, while French and American writers made little use of it until the late eighteenth century. This does not necessarily mean that British writers were more intelligent and up-to-date,

---

Filmer: Robert Filmer (c. 1588–1653) was a seventeenth-century English writer whose *Patriarcha* (1680) justified monarchy as the only legitimate source of political authority.

but is probably due to the fact that in British history the seventeenth century was the time of storm and stress for kings, whereas this time fell later in France and America. Jefferson used the compact theory to justify revolution just as Locke did: the theory came with the revolution in both cases. Rousseau was indeed not justifying an actual revolution; but, as Chateaubriand said, the Revolution in France "was accomplished before it occurred." It was accomplished in men's minds before they made it the work of their hands; and Rousseau spoke for all those who were "intending their minds" away from an actual, irrational, and oppressive political order which rested in theory upon the divine right of kings and priests to rule — and misrule. In all three countries this common influence — the widespread desire to limit the power of kings and priests — was one source of those underlying presuppositions which determined the character of political speculation in the eighteenth century; a strong antipathy to kings and priests predisposed Jefferson and Rousseau, as it predisposed Locke, to "intend their minds" towards some new sanction for political authority.

The idea that secular political authority rested upon compact was not new — far from it; and it had often enough been used to limit the authority of princes. It could scarcely have been otherwise indeed in that feudal age in which the mutual obligations of vassal and overlord were contractually conceived and defined. Vassals were often kings and kings often vassals; but all were manifestly vassals of God who was the Lord of lords and the King of kings. Thus mediaeval philosophers had conceived of the authority of princes as resting upon a compact with their subjects, a compact on their part to rule righteously, failing which their subjects were absolved from allegiance; but this absolution was commonly thought to become operative only through the intervention of the Pope, who, as the Vice-regent of God on earth, possessed by divine right authority over princes as well as over other men. Thus princes ruled by divine right after all, only their right was a secondhand right, deriving from God through the Pope. Afterwards the princes, when they had become kings and as kings had got the upper hand, jostled the Pope out of his special seat and became coequals with him in God's favor; so that in the seventeenth century the right of kings to rule was commonly thought to come directly from God, and the Pope lost his power of intervening to absolve subjects from allegiance to a bad king. Charles II of England and Louis XIV of France both thought this a reasonable doctrine, nor did either of them lack learned men to back them up; Bossuet* proved that it was obviously good religious doctrine — *Politique tirée de l'Écriture Sainte;* while Cambridge University assured Charles II that "Kings derive

---

Bossuet: Jacques-Bénigne Bossuet (1627–1704), a French bishop who defended the divine right of kings.

not their authority from the people but from God; . . . To Him only they are accountable."[5]

This clearly closed the door to relief in case there should be any bad kings. In the sixteenth and seventeenth centuries there were a number of bad kings; and so some people were always to be found seeking a method of bringing bad kings to book. Popular resistance to kings was commonly taught both by the Jesuits and the Protestant dissenters: by the Jesuits (by Catholic monarchists called "dissenters") on the ground that only the Pope has Divine authority; by Protestant Dissenters (by Protestant monarchists called "Jesuits") on the ground that it was possible for subjects themselves to claim as intimate relations with God as either king or Pope. Calvin was one of the writers who opened up this latter inviting prospect to succeeding generations.

> The first duty of subjects towards their rulers is to entertain the most honorable views of their office, recognizing it [the office not the king] as a delegated jurisdiction from God, and on that account receiving and reverencing them as the ministers and ambassadors of God.

This is admitted; but then the ambassador must clearly abide by his instructions; and therefore,

> In that obedience which we hold to be due to the commands of rulers we must . . . be particularly careful that it is not incompatible with obedience to Him to whose will the wishes of all kings should be subject. . . . The Lord, therefore, is King of Kings. . . . We are subject to men who rule over us, but subject only in the Lord. If they command anything against Him, let us not pay the least heed to it.[6]

What God had commanded, subjects might plainly read in holy writ — the scriptures as interpreted by those ministers whose business it was to understand them; for which reason, no doubt, Calvin would have ministers and magistrates walk together in close communion.

In 1579, another Frenchman, Hubert Languet, or whoever it was that wrote the *Vindiciae contra tyrannos*, gave greater precision to this idea. Subjects are obviously not bound to obey a king who commands what is contrary to the will of God. But are they bound to resist such a king? According to the *Vindiciae* they are. When kings were set up, two compacts were entered into: in the first, God on the one side, and people and king on the other, engaged to maintain the ancient covenant which God had formerly made with his chosen people of Israel; in the second, the king contracted with his subjects to rule justly, and they with him to be obedient.[7] Thus kings are under binding contract to rule justly, while subjects have a covenant with God to see that they do so. In the seventeenth century English sectaries not only preached but practiced resistance to kings and magistrates, finding their justification, not so much in an explicit compact with God, as in natural law, which was that right reason or inner light of conscience which God had given to men for their guidance. The Levellers* were complained of because, be the "Lawes and customes of a Kingdom never so plain and cleer against their wayes, yet they will not submit, but cry out for natural rights derived from Adam and right reason." Milton spoke for the refractory dissenters of that age when he said,

> There is no power but of God (Paul, *Rom.* 13), as much as to say, God put it in man's heart to find out that way at first for common peace and preservation, approving the exercise thereof. . . . For if it needs must be a sin in them to depose, it may as likely be a sin to have elected. And contrary, if the people's act in election be pleaded by a king, as the act of God and the most just title to enthrone him, why may not the people's act of rejection be as well pleaded by the people as the act of God, and the most just reason to depose him?[8]

Here was a "version of the original compact" which Locke might have used to justify the Revolution of 1688. He might have said, with any amount of elaboration, that the people had a compact with God which reserved to them the right to rebel when kings ruled unrighteously. Why was Locke not satisfied with this version? Certainly no one had less desire than Locke to deny that God was the maker and ruler of all. He could quote scripture too, as well as Milton or Filmer. We see, he says, that in the dispute between Jephthah and the Ammonites, "he [Jephthah] was forced to appeal to Heaven": "The Lord the Judge (says he) be judge this day." Well, of course, says Locke, "everyone knows that Jephthah here tells us, that the Lord the Judge shall judge."[9] But the trouble is the Lord does not do it now; he reserves his decision till the Day of Judgment. Jephthah appealed to the Lord, but the Lord did not speak, did not decide the dispute between Jephthah and the Ammonites; the result of which was that Jephthah had to decide it himself by leading out his armies. So it always is in the affairs of men: whether I shall appeal to Heaven, "I myself can only be the judge in my own conscience, as I will answer it, at the great day, to the supreme judge of all men." If we resist kings, God will no doubt judge us for it in the last day; but men will judge us now. Let us, therefore, ask whether there is not happily a compact between men and kings, God not interfering, on which we can stand to be judged by men when we resist kings.

Levellers: The Levellers were the most radical opponents of royal authority during the English Civil War of the 1640s.

The truth is that Locke, and the English Whigs, and Jefferson and Rousseau even more so, had lost that sense of intimate intercourse and familiar conversation with God which religious men of the sixteenth and seventeenth centuries enjoyed. Since the later seventeenth century, God had been withdrawing from immediate contact with men, and had become, in proportion as he receded into the dim distance, no more than the Final Cause, or Great Contriver, or Prime Mover of the universe; and as such was conceived as exerting his power and revealing his will indirectly through his creation rather than directly by miraculous manifestation or through inspired books. In the eighteenth century as never before, 'Nature' had stepped in between man and God; so that there was no longer any way to know God's will except by discovering the 'laws' of Nature, which would doubtless be the laws of 'nature's god' as Jefferson said. "Why should I go in search of Moses to find out what God has said to Jean Jacques Rousseau?" Why indeed, when the true revelation was all about him in Nature, with sermons in stones, books in the running brooks, and God in everything. The eighteenth century, seeking a modified version of the original compact, had to find it in nature or forever abandon the hope of finding it.

The concept of Nature was of course nothing new either, any more than the theory of compact. Stoic philosophers and Roman jurists had made much of Nature and Natural Law. Thomas Aquinas, in the thirteenth century, noted three distinct meanings of the word natural as applied to man. The third of these meanings, which mediaeval writers had taken over from the classical world, Aquinas defines as "an inclination in man to the good, according to the *rational* nature which is proper to him; as, for example, man has a natural inclination to know the truth about God, and to live in society." Natural law was accordingly that part of law discoverable by right reason, and as such occupied a strictly subordinate place in the mediaeval hierarchy of laws. According to Aquinas, the highest of all laws, comprehending all others, was the Eternal Law, which was nothing less than the full mind of God. Something, but not all, of the mind of God could be known to man: part of it had been revealed in the Bible or might be communicated through the Church (Positive Divine Law); and part of it could be discovered by human reason (Natural Law); lowest of all in the hierarchy came Human Law, or the positive laws of particular states.[10] Thus Natural Law obviously took precedence over Human Law, but must always be subordinate to that part of the Eternal Law which God had revealed in the Bible or through the Church. Natural Law was in fact not the law of nature, but a natural method of learning about the law of God. Above all, what could be learned by this method was strictly limited: Natural Law was that part of the mind of God which man could discover by using his reason, but God had provided beforehand, through the Bible and the Church, a sure means of letting man know when his reason was not right reason but unreason.

The concept of Nature which held the field in the eighteenth century seems at first sight very different from this; but the difference is after all mainly on the surface. The eighteenth century did not abandon the old effort to share in the mind of God; it only went about it with greater confidence, and had at last the presumption to think that the infinite mind of God and the finite mind of man were one and the same thing. This complacent view of the matter came about partly through the Protestant Reformation, which did much to diminish the authority of the Church as the official interpreter of God's will; but it came about still more through the progress of scientific investigation which had been creating, since the time of Copernicus, a strong presumption that the mind of God could be made out with greater precision by studying the mechanism of his created universe than by meditating on the words of his inspired prophets. Some of the 'laws' of this curious mechanism had already been formulated by Kepler and Galileo. Well, what if all the 'laws' of God's universe could be discovered by the human reason? In that case would not the infinite mind of God be fully revealed, and the Natural Law be identical with the Eternal Law? Descartes was bold enough to suggest this wonderful possibility. "I think, therefore, I am." Whatever is, is rational; hence there is an exact correspondence between human reason and the objective world. I think, therefore I am; and if I can think straight enough and far enough, I can identify myself with all that is. This 'all that is' the eighteenth century understood as Nature; and to effect a rational explanation of the relation and operation of all that is, was what it meant by discovering the 'laws' of Nature. No doubt Natural Law was still, as in the time of Aquinas, that part of the mind of God which a rational creature could comprehend; but if a rational creature could comprehend all that God had done, it would, for all practical purposes, share completely the mind of God, and the Natural Law would be, in the last analysis, identical with the Eternal Law. Having deified Nature, the eighteenth century could conveniently dismiss the Bible and drop the concept of Eternal Law altogether. . . .

The eighteenth century, obviously, did not cease to bow down and worship; it only gave another form and a new name to the object of worship: it deified Nature and denatured God. Since Nature was now the new God, source of all wisdom and righteousness, it was to Nature that the eighteenth century looked for guidance, from Nature that it expected to receive the tablets of the law; and it was just as necessary now as ever for the mind of the rational creature to share in the mind of this new God, in order that his conduct, including the "positive laws of particular states," might conform to the universal purpose. The Philosopher, as Maclaurin says, "while he contemplates and admires so excellent a System, *cannot but be himself excited and animated to correspond with the general harmony of Nature.*" The words may be taken as a just expression of the eighteenth century state of mind: on its knees, with uplifted eyes contemplating and admiring the Universal Order, it was excited and animated to correspond with the general harmony.

This was no doubt an inspiring idea, but certainly not a new one. Great and good men in all ages had endeavored to correspond with the general harmony. Formerly this was conceived as an endeavor to become one with God; and for some centuries the approved method, in Europe, was thought to be fasting and prayer, the denial of the flesh, the renunciation of the natural man. "Who shall deliver me from the body of this death!" cried the saint. The physical and material world was thought to be a disharmony, a prison house, a muddy vesture of decay, closing in and blinding the spirit so that it could not enter into the harmony that was God. But the eighteenth century, conceiving of God as known only through his work, conceived of his work as itself a universal harmony, of which the material and the spiritual were but different aspects.

In breaking down the barriers between the material and the spiritual world, between man and nature, John Locke played a great role. His *Essay Concerning the Human Understanding,* published in 1690, was an enquiry into "the original, certainty, and extent of human knowledge," an enquiry which the author thought of the highest use "since it is the understanding that sets man above the rest of sensible beings, and gives him all the advantage and dominion which he has over them." The first part of this enquiry was devoted to "ideas," and "how they come into the mind." On this point Locke thought he had something new to say, and his first task was to show how untenable the currently accepted view was.

> It is an established opinion amongst some men, that there are in the *understanding* certain *innate principles,* some primary notions . . . stamped upon the mind of man, which the soul receives in its very first being, and brings into the world with it. It would be sufficient to convince unprejudiced readers of the falseness of this supposition, if I should only show . . . how men, barely by the use of their natural faculties, may attain to all the knowledge they have, without the help of any innate impressions. . . . For I imagine any one will easily grant that it would be impertinent to suppose the ideas of colours innate in a creature, to whom God hath given sight and power to receive them by the eyes, from external objects: and no less unreasonable would it be to attribute several truths to the impressions of nature, and innate characters, when we may observe in ourselves faculties fit to attain as easy and certain knowledge of them, as if they were originally imprinted on the mind.[11]

Although this alone, Locke thought, ought to convince a reasonable man, he nevertheless devoted sixty pages of fine print to proving that there is no such thing as an innate idea; and having demonstrated this point, he devoted more pages still to proving that "all ideas come from sensation or reflection."

> Let us then suppose the mind to be, as we say, white paper, void of all characters, without any *ideas;* how comes it to be furnished? . . . To this I answer, in one word, from *experience;* in that all our knowledge is founded, and from that it ultimately derives itself. Our observation employed either about *external sensible objects, or about the internal operations of our minds, perceived and reflected on by ourselves, is that which supplies our understanding with all the materials of thinking.* These two are the fountains of knowledge, from which all the ideas we have, or can naturally have, do spring.[12]

Of these two fountains of knowledge, the more important was the first — impressions received from external sensible objects. This "great source of most of the ideas we have, depending wholly upon our senses, and derived from them to the understanding, I call SENSATION."

Locke's "sensational" philosophy became, with some modifications in detail, the psychological gospel of the eighteenth century. A trained philosopher might think that the conception of 'innate ideas' which Locke destroyed was no more than a man of straw, a "theory of innate ideas," as Mr. Webb says, "so crude that it is difficult to suppose any serious thinker ever held it."[13] That may be. Yet it is certain that Locke's book had a great influence on the common thought of his age, which may be due to the fact that serious thinkers are few, while crude theories, generally speaking, rule the world. Put in the form in which it entered into the common thought of the eighteenth century, Locke's theory may be stated as follows: God has not revealed the truth that is necessary for man's guidance, once for all, in holy writ, or stamped upon the minds of all men certain intuitively perceived intellectual and moral ideas which correspond to the truth so revealed; on the contrary, all the ideas we can have come from experience, are the result of the sensations that flow in upon us from the natural and social world without, and of the operations of the reflecting mind upon these sensations; from which it follows that man, as a thinking and an acting creature, is part and parcel of the world in which he lives, intimately and irrevocably allied to that Universal Order which is at once the work and the will of God.

Locke's *Essay Concerning the Human Understanding* went into the 26th edition in 1828. There is in existence a copy of this edition which contains an autograph letter from Andrew Lang to a friend: "Dear Grose, This is yours; I never read one word of Mr. Locke, but how did the dreary devil stagger like Crockett to a 26th edition?"[14] The answer to this question is that most of the twenty-six editions were printed in the eighteenth century, and the eighteenth century prized Locke because he furnished a formal argument in support of the idea that "men, *barely by the use of their natural faculties,* may attain to all the knowledge they have." Locke, more perhaps than any one else, made it possible for the eighteenth century to believe what it wanted to believe: namely, that in the world of human relations as well as in the physical world, it was possible for men to "correspond with the general harmony of Nature"; that since man, and the mind of man, were integral parts of the work of God, it was possible for man, by the use of his mind, to bring his thought and conduct, and hence the institutions by which he lived, into a perfect harmony with the Universal Natural Order. In the eighteenth century, therefore, these truths were widely accepted as self evident: that a valid morality would be a 'natural morality,' a valid religion would be a 'natural religion,' a valid law of politics would be a 'natural law.' This was only another way of saying that morality, religion, and politics ought to conform to God's will as revealed in the essential nature of man.

It went without saying that kings and ministers and priests, as well as philosophers, ought to be "excited and animated to correspond with the general harmony of Nature"; and if, once fully enlightened on that point, they would not do so, they must unquestionably be pronounced no better than rebels against the Great Contriver, and Author and Governor of the Universe. But how, after all, could you tell for sure whether kings and ministers and priests were, or were not, in accord with Nature? The presumption was no doubt against them, but how be sure? In appealing from custom and positive law to the overruling law of God, the eighteenth century followed well-established precedent; but a practical difficulty arose when the will of God was thought to be revealed, neither in papal command nor in the words of scripture, but in the endless, half-deciphered Book of Nature. Nature was doubtless an open book, yet difficult to read, and likely to convey many meanings, so various a language did it speak. George III, as well as Sam Adams, was presumably God's work; and if God's will was revealed in his work, how were you to know that the acts of George III, whose nature it was to be tyrannical, were not in accord with Natural Law, while the acts of Sam Adams, whose nature it was to be fond of Liberty, were in accord with Natural Law? Everything in the physical world was certainly part of God's universe, and therefore according to nature; why was not everything in the world of human relations part of God's universe also, and equally according to nature?

It was easy enough to read the Book of Nature in this sense, and even to make verse out of it, as Pope did.

> All are but parts of one stupendous whole,
> Whose body Nature is, and God the soul; . . .

All Nature is but art, unknown to thee;
All chance, direction, which thou canst not see;
All discord, harmony not understood;
All partial evil, universal good:
And, spite of pride, in erring reason's spite,
One truth is clear, whatever is, is right.

According to this reading it seemed that Nature, having devoured God, was on the point of incontinently swallowing Man also — a monstrous conclusion for those who were convinced that all was *not* right. That all was not right was a belief that became widespread and profoundly held in the latter eighteenth century; and those who were thus "steadily intending their minds" away from the actual political and social order in search of a better, had at all hazards to make out that certain aspects of actual human relations were not in harmony with Nature, while other aspects were. Convinced that the torture of Calas, for example, or the Stamp Act, or George III, was something less than "harmony not understood," they had to demonstrate that "life, liberty, and the pursuit of happiness" were according to Nature and the will of God, whereas tyranny and cruelty and the taking of property without consent were not.

This is only another way of saying that in order to find a fulcrum in Nature for moving the existing order, the eighteenth century had to fall back upon the commonplace distinction between good and bad; unless the will of God, as revealed in the nature of man, was to be thought of as morally indifferent, some part of this nature of man had to be thought of as good and some part as bad. The eighteenth century had to appeal, as it were, from nature drunk to nature sober. Now the test or standard by which this appeal could be validly made was found in nature itself — in reason and conscience; for reason and conscience were parts of man's nature too, and God had manifestly given man reason and conscience, as natural guides, precisely in order that he might distinguish that part of his own thought and conduct which was naturally good from that which was naturally bad. Natural law, as a basis for good government, could never be found in the undifferentiated nature of man, but only in human reason applying the test of good and bad to human conduct. Thus the eighteenth century, having apparently ventured so far afield, is nevertheless to be found within hailing distance of the thirteenth; for its conception of natural law in the world of human relations was essentially identical, as Thomas Aquinas' conception had been, with right reason.

It is true that right reason had a much freer field in the eighteenth century than in the thirteenth; it was not limited either by a special revelation or by an established Church; and above all it could appeal for support to history, to the experience of mankind. From the record of human activities in all times and in all places, as well as from the established laws of the material universe, it would be easily possible to verify and to substantiate the verdict of right reason. Whatever the Bible might say, right reason could reject miracles because they were contrary to common sense and the observed procedure of the physical world. Whatever the Church might command, right reason could denounce cruelty and intolerance because the common conscience of mankind revolted at cruelty and intolerance. Whatever the dogmas of particular religions might be, right reason could prefer the precepts of natural Religion which were to be found as Voltaire said, in the "principles of morality common to the human race." Whatever customs and positive laws might prevail in particular states, right reason could estimate their value in the light of the customs and laws common to all states. What I have searched for, said Montaigne, is "la connaissance de l'homme en général"— the knowledge of man in general.[15] This is precisely what the eighteenth century did: with the lantern of enlightenment it went up and down the field of human history looking for man in general, the universal man, man stripped of the accidents of time and place; it wished immensely to meet Humanity and to become intimate with the Human Race. If it could find Humanity it would have found man in general, the natural man; and so it would have some chance of knowing what were the rights and laws which, being suited to man in general, were most likely to be suited to particular men, everywhere and always.

We have now got a long way from the Declaration of Independence and Thomas Jefferson, and even from John Locke, in whose book Jefferson found so well expressed the ideas which he put into the Declaration. Let us then return to John Locke, whom we have too long left to his own devices, seeking a "modified form of the original compact," being unable to make use of the older version. The older version, which was a compact between the people and God in person, Locke could not use because, as we saw, nature had stepped in between God and man. Locke, like every one else, had therefore to make his way, guided by reason and conscience, through Nature to find the will of God; and the only version of the original compact from which he could derive governmental authority, was such a compact as men, acting according to their nature, would enter into among themselves. Since the will of God was revealed in Nature, you could find out what God had willed governments to be and do only by consulting Nature — the nature of man. The question which Locke had to answer was therefore this: What kind of political compact would men enter into, if they acted according to the nature which God had given them?

To answer this question, Locke says, we must consider

What state all men are naturally in, and that is, a state of perfect freedom to order their actions and dispose of their possessions and persons, as they think fit, within the bounds of the law of nature, without asking leave, or depending upon the leave of any other man. A state also of equality, wherein all power and jurisdiction is reciprocal, no one having more than another.[16]

This state which all men are "naturally in," this state of nature, is not a state of licence; it is a state of perfect freedom and equality, but of freedom and equality only *"within the bounds of the law of nature."* What is this law of nature?

The state of nature has a law to govern it, which obliges every one: and *reason, which is that law,* teaches all mankind, who will but consult it, that being all equal and independent, no one ought to harm another in his life, health, liberty, or possessions. . . .

In transgressing the law of nature, the offender declares himself to live by another rule than that of *reason and common equity, which is that measure God has set to the actions of men.* . . .

A criminal, who having renounced *reason, the common rule and measure God hath given to mankind,* hath, by the unjust violence and slaughter he hath committed on one, declared war against all mankind.[17]

In Locke's state of nature all men are thus free and all are bound. Is not this a paradox? No, because the state of nature, in which Locke seeks the origin of government, is not the actual presocial state of history, but an imaginative state rationally constructed. Locke, like the political writers of the eighteenth century, was not concerned to know how governments had come to be what they were; what he wanted to know was whether there was any justification for their being what they were. "Man is born free, and is everywhere in chains," exclaimed Rousseau. "How was this change made? I do not know. What can make it legitimate? I believe I can answer that question."[18] This is the question Locke seeks to answer — what can justify governments in binding men by positive laws? In order to answer it he first asks what law would bind men if government, positive law, and custom were, conceivably, nonexistent? His answer is that in that case no law would bind them except the law of reason. Reason would bind them, because reason is the "common rule and measure God hath given to mankind"; reason would at once bind and make free; it would, as Locke says, *oblige* every one: but it would oblige them precisely in this, that it would teach them that all are perfectly free and equal and that no one "ought to harm another in his life, health, liberty, or possessions." Locke's natural law is the law of reason, its only compulsion is an intellectual compulsion, the relations which it prescribes such as would exist if men should follow reason alone.

Such a state as this, an ideal state, in which all men follow the law of reason and no compulsion is necessary — such a state never in fact existed. Therefore let us modify this hypothetical state, so as to bring it a little nearer the reality. Suppose a few men in this rational state, refusing to act rationally, violate the law of nature which is reason, by taking away the "life, health, liberty or possessions of another." What is to be done about it? In that case, Locke says, "the execution of the law of nature is . . . put into every man's hands, whereby every one has a right to punish the transgressor of the law, . . . but only . . . so far as calm reason and conscience dictate, what is proportionate to his transgression."[19] Any one who should, for example, commit a murder, might, according to the law of reason, be put to death. "Cain was so fully convinced, that every one had a right to slay such a criminal, that after the murder of his brother, he cries out: 'Every one that findeth me, shall slay me.' So plain was it writ in the hearts of mankind."[20] Thus in this new rational Garden of Eden every one is the executor of that natural law of reason which God has written in the hearts of men: if a Cain appears now and then, any one may take his life.

Now it may be, let us suppose so at all events, that a good many Cains will appear, so that all the Abels, the great majority who still live by reason, are in danger of their lives, and are at great inconvenience to defend them. And suppose further that all these rational and conscientious Abels, being a great majority, come together saying: Why should we all be forever going up and down to watch where many Cains come to strike? Go to, let us appoint a few to watch for all. The question is, how might these many Abels be supposed to proceed in this business? Would they not say: These few, whom we appoint to watch for us, that we may be safe in our lives, our health, our liberty, and our possessions, are to make what rules are necessary for that purpose, but for that purpose only; and we agree in return to abide by those rules, so long as the few whom we appoint to make the rules do effectively, by means of these rules, make us safe in our lives, our liberties, and our possessions. Such is the modified version of the original compact which Locke finds in the state of nature.

Men being, as has been said, all free, equal, and independent, no one can be put out of his estate, and subjected to the political power of another, without his consent. The only way, whereby any one divests himself of his liberty, and puts on the bonds of civil society, is by agreeing with other men to join and unite into a community, for their comfortable, safe, and peaceable living one amongst another, in a secure enjoyment of their properties, and a greater security against any, that are not of it. . . . When any number of men have so consented to make one community or government, they are thereby presently incorporated, and make one body politic, wherein the majority have a right to act and conclude the rest.[21]

This is all very well, in a hypothetical state of nature; but it might be asked, "it is often asked as a mighty objection, 'Where are, or ever were men in such a state of nature?'"[22] Well, they are so, Locke replies in substance, whenever they find themselves in relation without any positive law to bind them; as, for example, rulers of sovereign states in relation to each other, or the "two men on the desert island, mentioned by Garcilasso de la Vega in his history of Peru." These are in a state of nature "in reference to one another: for truth and keeping of faith belongs to men as men, and not to members of society." Men as *men* (that is to say man in the abstract, Montaigne's "man in general") are in the state of nature. Locke's state of nature is not the actual presocial state of history, but the logical nonsocial state, which he constructs imaginatively, as a premise from which to deduce the rational limits of governmental authority. In the actual presocial state of history there may well have been more Cains than Abels; and no doubt governments have in fact been established by custom unconsciously and irrationally submitted to, or by force, by conquest, or by the flagrant usurpation of kings. This is admitted; but the fact of tyranny is no more a justification of tyranny in the social state, than the fact of murder is a justification of murder in the presocial state. What Locke is seeking is not the historical origin, but the rational justification, of government.

If, therefore, any one says that men never did in fact live in a state where conduct was guided by reason, but that in fact they originally lived in a state of confusion and anarchy, in a state of war, and that "therefore God hath certainly appointed government to restrain the partiality and violence of men," the answer is that this is no doubt true. But what do you deduce from this truth? Do you say that because God has appointed governments to restrain the violence of men, it follows that God approves of tyrannical governments because tyrannical governments do in fact exist? If you say so, then you say, with Hobbes, that God approves any government which gets itself established because it gets itself established, and in so far as it has power to maintain itself. Well, Locke says, I do not agree with you.

> I easily grant, that civil government is the proper remedy for the inconveniences of the state of nature, which must certainly be great where men may be judges in their own case: . . . but I shall desire those who make this objection, to remember, that absolute monarchs are but men; and if government is to be the remedy of those evils, which necessarily follow from men's being judges in their own cases, and the state of nature is therefore not to be endured; I desire to know what kind of government that is, and how much better it is than the state of nature, where one man commanding a multitude, has the liberty to be judge in his own case, and may do to all his subjects whatever he pleases, without the least liberty to any one to question or control those who execute his pleasure?[23]

The sum and substance of Locke's elaborate enquiry into the origin and character of government is this: since reason is the only sure guide which God has given to men, reason is the only foundation of just government; and so I ask, not what authority any government has in fact, but what authority it ought in reason to have; and I answer that it ought to have the authority which reasonable men, living together in a community, considering the rational interests of each and all, might be disposed to submit to willingly; and I say further that unless it is to be assumed that any existing government has of right whatever authority it exercises in fact, then there is no way of determining whether the authority which it exercises in fact is an authority which it exercises of right, except by determining what authority it ought in reason to have. Stripped of its decorative phrases, of its philosophy of 'Nature' and 'Nature's God' and the 'Universal Order,' the question which Locke asked was a simple one: "I desire to know what kind of government that is . . . where one man . . . many do to all his subjects whatever he pleases, without the least liberty to any one to question or control those who execute his pleasure?" This, generally speaking, was what the eighteenth century desired to know. The answer which it gave to that question seemed self-evident: Such a government is a bad government; since governments exist for men, not men for governments, all governments derive their just powers from the consent of the governed.

If the philosophy of Locke seemed to Jefferson and his compatriots just 'the common sense of the matter,' it was not because Locke's argument was so lucid and cogent that it could be neither misunderstood nor refuted. Locke's argument is not particularly cogent unless you accept his assumptions as proved, nor lucid until you restate it to suit yourself; on the contrary, it is lumbering, involved, obscured by innumerable and conflicting qualifications — a dreary devil of an argument staggering from assumption posited as premise to conclusion implicit in the assumption. It was Locke's conclusion that seemed to the colonists sheer common sense, needing no argument at all. Locke did not need to convince the colonists because they were already convinced; and they were already convinced because they had long been living under governments which did, in a rough and ready way, conform to the kind of government for which Locke furnished a reasoned foundation. The colonists had never in fact lived under a government where "one man . . . may do to all his subjects whatever he pleases." They were accustomed to living under governments which proceeded, year by year, on a tacitly assumed compact between rulers and ruled, and which were in fact very largely dependent upon "the consent of the governed." How should the colonists not accept a philosophy, however clumsily argued, which assured them that their own governments, with which they were well content, were just the kind that God had designed men by nature to have!

The general philosophy which lifted this common sense conclusion to the level of a cosmic law, the colonists therefore accepted, during the course of the eighteenth century, without difficulty, almost unconsciously. That human conduct and institutions should conform to the will of God was an old story, scarcely to be questioned by people whose ancestors were celebrated, in so many instances, for having left Europe precisely in order to live by God's law. Living by God's law, as it turned out, was much the same as living according to "the strong bent of their spirits." The strong bent of their spirits, and therefore God's law, had varied a good deal according to the locality, in respect to religion more especially; but so far as one could judge at this late enlightened date, God had showered his blessings indifferently upon all alike — Anglicans and Puritans, Congregationalists and Presbyterians, Catholics, Baptists, Shakers and Mennonites, New Lights and Old Lights. Even Quakers, once thought necessary to be hanged as pestilent blasphemers and deniers of God's will, now possessed a rich province in peace and content. Many chosen peoples had so long followed God's law by relying upon their own wits, without thereby running into destruction, that experience seemed to confirm the assertion that nature was the most reliable revelation of God's will, and human reason the surest interpreter of nature.

The channels through which the philosophy of Nature and Natural Law made its way in the colonies in the eighteenth century were many. A good number of Americans were educated at British universities, where the doctrines of Newton and Locke were commonplaces; while those who were educated at Princeton, Yale, or Harvard could read, if they would, these authors in the original, or become familiar with their ideas through books of exposition. The complete works of both Locke and Newton were in the Harvard library at least as early as 1773. Locke's works were listed in the Princeton catalogue of 1760. As early as 1755 the Yale library contained Newton's *Principia* and Locke's *Essay;* and before 1776 it contained the works of Locke, Newton, and Descartes, besides two popular expositions of the Newtonian philosophy. The revolutionary leaders do not often refer to the scientific or philosophical writings of either Newton or Locke, although an occasional reference to Locke's *Essay* is to be found; but the political writings of Locke, Sidney, and Milton are frequently mentioned with respect and reverence. Many men might have echoed the sentiment expressed by Jonathan Mayhew* in 1766:

> Having been initiated, in youth, in the doctrines of civil liberty, as they were taught by such men as Plato, Demosthenes, Cicero and other renowned persons among the ancients; and such as Sidney and Milton, Locke and Hoadley, among the moderns, I liked them; they seemed rational.[24]

Jonathan Mayhew: Mayhew (1720–1766) was a prominent New England minister who questioned royal authority as a vestige of papal despotism.

And Josiah Quincy expressed the common idea of his compatriots when, in 1774, he wrote into his will these words:

> I give to my son, when he shall arrive at the age of 15 years, Algernon Sidney's Works, John Locke's Works, Lord Bacon's Works, Gordon's Tacitus, and Cato's Letters. May the spirit of Liberty rest upon him![25]

For the general reader, the political philosophy of the eighteenth century was expounded from an early date in pamphlet and newspaper by many a Brutus, Cato, or Popliocola. An important, but less noticed, channel through which the fundamental ideas of that philosophy — God, Nature, Reason — were made familiar to the average man, was the church. Both in England and America preachers and theologians laid firm hold of the Newtonian conception* of the universe as an effective weapon against infidelity. Dr. Richard Bentley studied Newton in order to preach a "Confusion of Atheism," deriving a proof of Divine Providence from the physical construction of the universe as demonstrated by that "divine theorist," Sir Isaac Newton.[26] What a powerful support to Revelation (and to Revolution) was that famous argument from design! The sermons of the century are filled with it — proving the existence and the goodness of God from the intelligence which the delicately adjusted mechanism of Nature everywhere exhibited.[27]

In 1750 there was published at Boston a book of Twenty Sermons, delivered in the Parish Church at Charleston, South Carolina, by the Reverend Samuel Quincy. In these sermons we find the Nature philosophy fully elaborated.

> For a right knowledge of God by the Light of Nature, displays his several amiable Perfections; acquaints us with the Relation he stands in to us, and the Obligations we owe to him. . . . It teaches us that our greatest Interest and Happiness consists in loving and fearing God, and in doing his Will; that to imitate his moral Perfections in our whole Behaviour, is acting up to the Dignity of our Natures, and that he has endowed us with Reason and Understanding (Faculties which the Brutes have not) on purpose to contemplate his Beauty and Glory, and to keep our inferior Appetites in due Subjection to his Laws, written in our Hearts.[28]

In his famous election sermon of 1754, Jonathan Mayhew uses this philosophy, without the formulae, for deriving the authority of government. Government, he says,

---

Newtonian conception: Sir Isaac Newton (1642–1727) proposed that God had created the universe to operate according to natural principles that were discoverable by human reason. Once set in motion, the universe ran itself.

is both the ordinance of God, and the ordinance of man: of God, in respect to his original plan, and universal Providence; of man, as it is more immediately the result of human prudence, wisdom and concert.[29]

In later Massachusetts election sermons, from 1768 to 1773, we find both the philosophy and the formulae; the three concepts of God, Nature, and Reason, which Samuel Quincy made the foundation of religion, are there made the foundation of politics and government as well.[30] And so there crept into the mind of the average man this conception of Natural Law to confirm his faith in the majesty of God while destroying his faith in the majesty of Kings.

English writers in the nineteenth century, perhaps somewhat blinded by British prejudice against the French Revolution and all its works, complacently took it for granted that the political philosophy of Nature and natural rights upon which the Revolution was founded, being particularly vicious must be peculiarly French; from which it followed, doubtless as the night the day, that the Americans, having also embraced this philosophy, must have been corrupted by French influence. The truth is that the philosophy of Nature, in its broader aspects and in its particular applications, was thoroughly English. English literature of the seventeenth and eighteenth centuries is steeped in this philosophy. The Americans did not borrow it; they inherited it. The lineage is direct: Jefferson copied Locke and Locke quoted Hooker. In political theory and in political practice the American Revolution drew its inspiration from the parliamentary struggle of the seventeenth century. The philosophy of the Declaration was not taken from the French. It was not even new; but good old English doctrine newly formulated to meet a present emergency. In 1776 it was commonplace doctrine, everywhere to be met with, as Jefferson said, "whether expressed in conversation, in letters, printed essays, or the elementary books of public right." And in sermons also, he might have added. But it may be that Jefferson was not very familiar with sermons.

Notes

1. *Works of John Adams,* II, 512.
2. *The Writings of Thomas Jefferson* (ed. 1869), VII, 304.
3. Ibid., 407.
4. *History of the Science of Politics,* 65.
5. *History of Passive Obedience,* 108.
6. *Institutes of Christianity,* Bk. IV, Ch. 20, sec. 22, 32.
7. *Vindiciae contra tyrannos* (ed. 1579), 55.
8. "Tenure of Kings and Magistrates"; *Works of John Milton* (Mitford ed., 1851), IV, 464, 465.
9. "Of Civil Government," Bk. II, sec. 21; *Works of John Locke* (ed. 1812), V, 350.

10. Quoted in Richie, *Natural Rights*, 39.

11. Locke, *Essay* (ed. 1813), I, 42.

12. Ibid., 97, 98.

13. Webb, C. J., *Studies in the History of Natural Theology*, 354.

14. Autograph letter quoted in Sotheran's secondhand book catalogue, No. 61, p. 31.

15. Quoted in Faguet, *XVIme siècle*, 371.

16. "Of Civil Government," Bk. II, sec. 4; *Works* (ed. 1812).

17. Ibid., sec. 6, 8, 11.

18. *Du contract social, ou principes du droit politique* (ed. 1762), 2.

19. "Of Civil Government," Bk. II, sec. 8.

20. Ibid., sec. 11.

21. Ibid., sec. 95.

22. Ibid., sec. 14.

23. Ibid., sec. 13.

24. *The Patriot Preachers of the American Revolution*, 39.

25. Rosenthal, "Rousseau at Philadelphia"; *Magazine of American History*, XII, 54.

26. Brewster, D., *Memoirs of Sir Isaac Newton*, I, 340. Wheewell, *Inductive Sciences*, I, 421.

27. For an admirable statement of the argument, see Hume, "Dialogue on Natural Religion"; *Works* (Green ed.), II, 393.

28. Quincy, *Twenty Sermons*, 59, 60.

29. *A Sermon Preached in the Audience of His Excellency William Shirley, Esq., May 29, 1754*, p. 2.

30. *A Sermon Preached before His Excellency Francis Bernard, May 25, 1768*, By Daniel Shute. Boston, 1768. *A Sermon Preached . . . May 31, 1769*, By Jason Haven. Boston, 1769. *A Sermon . . . May 30, 1770*, By Samuel Cooke. Boston, 1770. *A Sermon . . . May 29, 1771*, By Frederick Tucker. Boston, 1771. *A Sermon . . . May 27, 1772*, By Moses Parsons. Boston, 1772.

3. Or was Jefferson more influenced by Scottish thinkers?

Garry Wills

Jefferson and the Scottish Enlightenment

From *Inventing America: Jefferson's Declaration of Independence*

Becker's interpretation of the philosophical sources that shaped the Declaration stood virtually unchallenged for over fifty years, influencing all scholarship on the subject, to include Dumas Malone's magisterial biography of Jefferson. The first serious criticism of the Lockean explanation came from Garry Wills. In the selection reprinted here, Wills questions the influence of Locke by examining the books and reading lists of young Jefferson and discovering that Scottish rather than English authors dominate the lists. If correct, Will's interpretation has far-reaching intellectual implications, for the Scottish Enlightenment made the "moral sense" the distinguishing human quality; it was less individualistic than collectivistic. Note, however, that both Becker and Wills consider the philosophy of the Declaration and the mind of Thomas Jefferson as synonymous, and both also explain Jefferson's mind in terms of the books he read.

Questions for a Closer Reading

1. What difference does it make whether English or Scottish ideas most influenced Jefferson?

2. What are the "Scottish ideas" that Wills sees as influencing the young Jefferson? How do these ideas differ from those of Locke?

3. Are there passages in Jefferson's original draft of the Declaration that change in meaning if Wills is correct?

4. What is the intellectual significance of what Wills calls "the problem of the Shadwill fire"?

5. Does Wills make a convincing case for the influence of William Small?

6. Think about the way that Wills constructs his argument *against* Lockean influence ("proving a negative"). What *evidence* does he base his conclusions on? How can historians finally settle this debate?

Jefferson and the Scottish Enlightenment

It was my great good fortune, and what probably fixed the destinies of my life, that Dr. William Small of Scotland was then Professor of Mathematics, a man profound in the most useful branches of science, with a happy talent of communication, correct and gentlemanly manners, and an enlarged and liberal mind. He, most happily for me, became soon attached to me, and made me his daily companion when not engaged in the school; and from his conversation I got my first views of the expansion of science, and of the system of things in which we are placed.
—JEFFERSON, *Autobiography*

One of the great blows to American scholarship took place on February 1, 1770, when a modest upland plantation burned to the ground. At the time, it was an entirely personal tragedy. The young master of Shadwell, Thomas Jefferson, was absent, and his mother was with him, so no lives were lost. But time would reveal what the world had lost: it had lost a world. Except for a few papers he carried with him — his account book, mainly, and two books of his private "florilegia"— this compulsive writer and record keeper lost everything he had composed to the age of twenty-seven, along with the library he had been assembling with great care and cost for over a decade.

The loss is easily put in concrete terms. Though the great Boyd edition

Garry Wills, *Inventing America: Jefferson's Declaration of Independence* (New York: Doubleday, 1978), 167–80.

of Jefferson's papers promises to stretch out to the crack of doom, only twenty-five pages of the first volume are devoted to his writings before the fire occurred — letters saved by their recipients (mainly John Page), one advertisement in the newspapers, one draft of a public paper.

That accident goes far toward explaining one of the odd things about Jeffersonian scholarship. Despite the fact that the Declaration of Independence is Jefferson's most influential composition, studies of his intellectual world tend to pick him up after 1776, when he wrote it. Daniel Boorstin, for instance, tries to reconstruct the "lost world" of Jefferson's thought around the Philadelphia activities of the American Philosophical Society, which Jefferson did not even join until 1780, and where he was not active for another decade — not, that is, until his Philadelphia years as Secretary of State and Vice President, the years when he turned fifty.

Other scholars pick Jefferson up, intellectually, when he reaches Paris (1784), in his forties. Gilbert Chinard (*Jefferson et les Idéologues,* 1925) and Adrienne Koch (*The Philosophy of Thomas Jefferson,* 1943) "place" him among the idéologues he knew and admired during and after his Paris sojourn. Useful as such studies may be for other purposes, they obviously tell us little about the formation of Jefferson during his prolonged stay in Williamsburg, when he laid the foundations of his vast reading and acquired his first views of the world.

The loss of Jefferson's earlier papers and books helps explain another oddity of Jeffersonian scholarship. That scholarship, so far as it touches on the intellectual sources of the Declaration, has stood virtually still for over half a century — ever since the publication of Carl Becker's little book on the subject. The foremost students of Jefferson have said, with surprising unanimity, that Becker's is the last word on this subject. Julian Boyd bowed to him at virtually every turn of his book on the evolution of the text:

> Mr. Becker's work contains a masterly analysis of the natural rights philosophy and of the American view of the nature of the British constitution. . . . I wish to acknowledge an indebtedness which all readers of this book must feel and which in my case is very great.

Malone relied as much on Becker's analysis (1 : 222–23), and William Peden spoke for his Jeffersonian mentors when he said: "Of all Jefferson's writings excepting the works published for the first time in this century, such as the Jefferson Bible and Chinard's editions of the Commonplace books, the Declaration of Independence alone has received what could properly be called authoritative and more or less final treatment. I have never heard anyone suggest that much of importance could be added to Carl Becker's book on the subject" (*Some Aspects of Jeffersonian Bibliography,* 1941).

What has made Becker's book so conclusive that even half a century later students of Jefferson found nothing important to add to it? It is true that Merrill Peterson could express misgivings about Becker's own relativism (*The Jefferson Image,* 308); but he had to concede, nonetheless, that Becker remained "the outstanding interpreter of the Declaration's philosophy" and his book was "a small masterpiece" (305). The secret of this universal acclaim lies in the inability of any later student to challenge Becker's basic thesis — that Jefferson found in *John Locke* "the ideas which he put into the Declaration."

You see how convenient this is. If we assume that there was a Lockean orthodoxy in the air, coloring all men's thoughts about politics in the middle of the eighteenth century, we do not have to worry much about the loss of Jefferson's own first lucubrations on the state, whatever philosophical jottings went up in flames when Shadwell burned. This assumption has, therefore, held its ground even though the public philosophy foisted, thus, on Jefferson conflicts with the private morality attributed to him by those who find his "lost world" in the moral-sense views of Philadelphians or the sociology of idéologues. Some people have noted this inconcinnity (e.g., Cecelia Kenyon and Morton White); but they explain it by saying that Jefferson later changed his mind — from the individualism of the (Lockean) Declaration to later communitarian values and morality. All such constructions rest on the certainty that Jefferson's first thoughts on politics *had* to be Lockean. But did they? There is, among modern Locke scholars, a heretical tendency to doubt that eighteenth-century politics had an orthodoxy derived from their man.

Locke's *Essay Concerning the True Original, Extent, and End of Civil Government,* known as the *Second Treatise,* written in the seventeenth century, was one of the canonical books of nineteenth-century liberalism. This has led us, looking back through the period of John Mill and David Ricardo, to forget how equivocal was the work's status in the eighteenth century. For the generally educated man or woman of today, Locke has become pre-eminently the man of the *Second Treatise* and only incidentally the author of the *Essay on Understanding.* In the eighteenth century, exactly the opposite was true. The *Essay,* by shaping the Enlightenment, had reshaped the world. The *Two Treatises,* appearing anonymously, had taken eighty years to make their mark in the English-speaking world, and never had much impact on the continent of Europe. Even when the *Second Treatise* became a standard work, it was at first revered because of its connection with the author of the *Essay.* Locke had original things to say in the *Second Treatise,* but they were not grasped or emphasized. His glorious name was just added to the list of authors in the whig tradition.

The work which best traces the spread of the *Second Treatise's* influence and editions is John Dunn's seminal essay of 1969, "The Politics of Locke in England and America in the Eighteenth Century" (in J. W. Yolton's *John Locke: Problems and Prospectives*). Dunn notes that Locke was even less known and studied in America than in England during the first half of the eighteenth century. Here too, the "great Mr. Locke" was Locke of the *Essay*. The impact of that work on Jonathan Edwards and Benjamin Franklin is well known. There is no similar epiphany traceable to the day when an American picked up the *Second Treatise*. The book was not much quoted until the eve of the Revolution, when men brought out all available spokesmen for the "whig" attack on absolutism. As Dunn puts it:

> There is no evidence that the *Two Treatises* figured in the set curriculum of any American college before the Revolution. . . . It never held the unimpeachable eminence of the works of Grotius or Pufendorf. . . . The book was of no great popularity before 1750, and the tradition of political behavior within which the colonists conceived their relationship with England was already highly articulated by this date. . . . It was only one among a large group of other works which expounded the Whig theory of the Revolution, and its prominence within this group is not noticeable until well after the general outline of the interpretation had become consolidated. [pp. 70–80]

The *great* Mr. Locke was the one who figured in that major trinity of the Enlightenment — Bacon, Newton, and Locke. It was a lesser figure who rounded out the lower triad of "Commonwealthmen" (as Caroline Robbins has called them) — Sidney, Harrington, and Locke.

Support for Dunn's argument can be gleaned from the survey of colonial and Early American libraries by David Lundberg and Henry F. May (*American Quarterly,* 1976). Copies of the 1814 edition of Locke's works can be found, at some point before 1776, in 23 percent of the known colonial libraries; but the distribution of interest in the different volumes of those works is measured by the fact that separate volumes of the *Treatise*(s) show up in only 15 percent of the libraries, while separate copies of the *Essay* were in 41 percent. Even in the politicized period from 1776 to 1790, when Dunn finds more interest in Locke's politics, appearance of the *Treatise* only went up to 24 percent (well behind, e.g., Montesquieu's *Spirit of the Laws* at 48 percent), while the *Essay* climbed to 62 percent. After 1790, the *Essay* continues popular while the *Treatise* dwindles drastically to 4 percent in the period 1790–1800, 2 percent (one copy!) in the period to 1813. This is hardly the "omnipresent" political Locke of our national myth.

Locke was, for men of Jefferson's period, the Newton of the mind — the man who revealed the workings of knowledge, the proper mode of education, and the reasonableness of belief. The most vivid and traceable influence Locke had on Jefferson was in the area of religious tolerance (*Papers,*

1:544–51). Elsewhere, when Jefferson refers to Locke, it is to his role in the major Enlightenment trinity, where the contribution was epistemological. He sought both busts and paintings of Bacon, Newton, and Locke — and drew an oval design to contain all three (*Papers,* 14:467–68, 525, 561).

When Jefferson refers to Locke's politics, he links him, not with Bacon and Newton, but invariably with Sidney.* The two were catalogued together in his own library (Sowerby, 3:12) and cited together in the list for a basic library (*Papers,* 1:79), for law readings (Ford, 9:480), and for the University of Virginia's curriculum. They lead the list of works on the rights of man, "for want of a single work" (Ford, 9:71). These recommendations fully accord with Dunn's argument that Locke was seen as a typical antiabsolutist of the whig tradition, without very specific reference to his originality. Locke was the Newton of the mind, not of the state.

Nowhere is the casual nature of Jefferson's references to Locke more evident than in the one place where he expressly links Locke with the Declaration. Repudiating the charge that he had plagiarized Locke, Jefferson wrote of his document: "All its authority rests then on the harmonizing sentiments of the day, whether expressed in conversation, in letters, printed essays, or in the elementary books of public right, as Aristotle, Cicero, Locke, Sidney, etc., &c." (Ford, 10:343). Four things are interesting in this 1814 passage: (1) The only time Jefferson links Locke's name with the Declaration, he is minimizing a connection first brought up by another. (2) He makes the customary pairing of Locke with Sidney as types of the whig ancestry claimed for the Revolution. (3) He is deliberately citing works of general regard, rather than a set of specific influences on him. (4) The latter point is confirmed by the inclusion of Aristotle, not one of Jefferson's favorite authors. He had a low regard for Geek metaphysicians in general (Cappon, 433) and for Aristotle's politics specifically:

> I think little edification can be obtained from their writings on the subject of government . . . [which] relieves our regret if the political writings of Aristotle or of any other ancient have been lost (Lipscomb and Bergh, 16:15).

Dunn notes that Locke was not considered a very practical guide by the very colonists who quoted him vaguely on matters of principle. Dr. Benjamin Rush, for instance, wrote in his *Observations on the Government of Pennsylvania:* "Mr. Locke is an oracle as to the principles, Harrington and Montesquieu are the oracles as to the forms of government." That rubric would also

---

Sidney: Algernon Sidney (1622–1683), an Englishman hanged for treason in 1683 on the grounds that he rejected the royal prerogative.

cover what is perhaps the highest praise ever given to Locke's *Treatise* by Jefferson: "Locke's little book on Government is perfect as far as it goes. Descending from theory to practice, there is no better book than the Federalist" (*Papers*, 16:449).

There is little in such references, scattered through his large body of writings, to justify the picture of Jefferson as a close student of Locke's politics. Yet Herbert Friedenwald* spoke for many others, down to our day, when he claimed that the Declaration "repeated the concepts, often even the very phraseology and arguments, of his master John Locke. . . . A reading of Locke's *Second Treatise* will show how thoroughly every sentence and expression in it were graven on Jefferson's mind" (*Declaration*, 201). It is not unusual to read that the Declaration "echoes" the *Treatise;* yet no precise verbal parallels have been adduced.[1] There is, indeed, no demonstrable verbal echo of the *Treatise* in all of Jefferson's vast body of writings. That general absence is striking enough; but the failure to use Locke in particular places is even more puzzling. The Declaration was written early in Jefferson's public career, not long after the deep course of political study traceable in his *Commonplace Book* and the so-called *Literary Bible*. In those books Jefferson copied out by hand long extracts from the standard authors (e.g., Montesquieu) and from private favorites (e.g., Bolingbroke). Yet there is not a single passage, in either book, copied out of Locke's *Treatise* — a book Jefferson never quoted in all his written remains!

There is one citation of the *Treatise* (not a quotation from it) in the *Commonplace Book*. But it is probably derived at second hand. It occurs in Jefferson's survey of governments and their forms, a survey derived from multiple sources. When Jefferson assembles the evidence for grounding the authority of kings in election, he appends a reference to the eleventh chapter of the *Treatise* on legislative supremacy — which is not the same matter at all. Apparently some reference in his reading made him think this citation apropos. Although the *Commonplace Book* has later additions and expansions, Jefferson never explained or corrected this reference.

The survey of governments in the *Commonplace Book* follows on the long extracts devoted to laws of property, a matter of consuming interest to Jefferson as well as Locke. It is hard to imagine that Jefferson could find no pertinent passages to quote or cite if he had his Locke at hand while working on this problem. Most of his later ideas on private property (107–20), entail (137–49), and inheritance (149–68) are traceable to the passages quoted here from Lord Kames and Sir John Dalrymple. Locke is never ad-

---

Herbert Friedenwald: A contemporary of Jefferson's.

duced; and if Locke is not relevant here, how can he be counted the major influence — or even *a* major influence — on Jefferson's political thinking?

The nature of the omission is best appreciated by noting that the very chapter of Locke cited once by Jefferson begins, "The great end of men's entering into society being the enjoyment of their properties . . ." and goes on to argue that taxation is never legitimate "without the consent of the people." If Jefferson had been reading Locke at this point, he would have had many appropriate passages to cite, instead of the one inappropriate reference he made.

There is no indication Jefferson read the *Second Treatise* carefully or with profit. Indeed, there is no direct proof he ever read it at all (though I assume he did at some point). There would be nothing dishonest about his general recommendation of the *Treatise*, made to others while he lacked any close acquaintance with the text — any more than in his crediting Aristotle (of all people) with formation of the background for his Declaration. Jefferson clearly had read, and admired, and learned from Locke's works on understanding, on education, on religious tolerance; and, like most of his contemporaries, he was willing to defer to the man's authority in politics without owing any specific debt to the *Treatise*.

We cannot look, for evidence that Jefferson read the *Treatise*, to his own copy of it, for no such copy exists. We know he ordered and received a copy of the *Treatise* late in 1769 (*Papers*, 1:33–34), but that volume perished almost immediately in the Shadwell fire. Jefferson listed the *Second Treatise* in his catalogue of books sold to the Library of Congress in 1815, but it does not show up in the list of books received (Sowerby, 3:12). He could not have withheld the book, since Congress did not allow that (Peden, University of Virginia diss. 1942, p. 154), and it seems unlikely it would have been lost in the short time between his compilation of the catalogue and completion of the sale. In any event he did not replace the book, as he did so many others. The 1829 list of his final library shows he had not owned the book since 1815 — and perhaps he had not owned it since the fire of 1770.

A possible explanation for the missing *Treatise* of the sale comes from the way Locke was regularly linked with Filmer, whom he refuted. Jefferson lists the *Treatise* right after two separately mentioned works of Filmer — but those Filmer works are bound together, in a neat leather book Sowerby thinks was purchased as part of Richard Bland's library in 1776. The first book included is a 1696 collection of Filmer's political tracts, whose table of contents lists as its sixth and final tract the *Patriarcha*. But that tract has been shorn away from the 1696 volume, and an earlier version of the *Patriarcha* (from 1690) is bound in its place. The book, which I have handled, seems to fall into three parts, since it opens easily to the Y binding signature, which begins the fifth tract, *The Power of Kings.* A quick glance may have led Jefferson to think *this* was *Patriarcha: Or the Natural Power of Kings,* and that the thing bound in after it was not *Patriarcha,* but "Locke's little book" written (as he thought) to answer Filmer. That would explain his belief that he sold the book to Congress. But even if this guess (and it is no more) be rejected, the evidence of Jefferson's physical connection with the book remains slight.

Of course, there is no proving a negative here (that Jefferson *could* not have been influenced by Locke) — which is not my aim, anyway. All I assert is that we have no reason to keep assuming that a Lockean orthodoxy explains the early formation of Jefferson's political thought. That short cut is no longer self-evidently valid. We must do the harder and slower work of trying to reassemble from fragments the world almost entirely lost in the Shadwell fire.

There *are* fragments to work on — the early parts of Jefferson's "florilegia," with their long extracts from Bolingbroke and Kames and Beccaria. And there is an important basic library list drawn up by Jefferson for a friend (Robert Skipwith) in 1771 — that is, in just the period when he was replacing his own lost library. His list indicates the core of the library Jefferson had first owned or aspired to own; and he told his friend that Monticello already held a more extensive collection than the 147 titles on the list. (That list is more extensive than the count of titles might indicate, since some of the single titles are things like "Milton's works" or "Dryden's plays"— *Papers,* 1:78.)

There are several interesting things about this list. One is the heavy component of novels and light literature, defended in the body of the letter in terms of a "moral sense" aesthetics — a trademark of such Scottish Enlightenment thinkers as Lord Kames. Kames, who figures so largely in the *Commonplace Book,* is represented in three different categories on the 1771 list — Law, Religion, and Criticism on the Fine Arts. He is only one of several Scots included — e.g., Adam Smith, Thomas Reid, David Hume (for both his essays and his history).

There should be nothing surprising in this concentration on Scottish thinkers. By the middle of the eighteenth century, Scotland's five universities had far outdistanced somnolent Oxford and Cambridge in the study of science, philosophy, and law. Edinburgh was replacing Leiden as the center of medical experiment and training. Glasgow had been renovated by the reforms of Francis Hutcheson. The two universities in Aberdeen were straining to catch up to the lead of Edinburgh and Glasgow. These schools had all thrown off the yoke of Dutch Calvinist professors just in time to adopt the new scientific outlook based on Newton and Locke. In the forties and fifties of the century, Scotland had a constellation of original thinkers not to be equaled anywhere in Europe — not only Hume and Smith, Kames and Hutcheson, but Adam Ferguson, Thomas Reid, and the young Dugald Stewart. Even before the publication of the *Wealth of Nations,* Scotland was known as the world's leader in the new field of "political economy." Scottish students were well trained in astronomy, mathematics, and the "mechanical" sciences. James Watt, the brilliant instrument-maker, found in Glasgow open-minded professors (Joseph Black and John Robison) who put him on the path toward perfecting the steam engine. The leadership that had been taken fifty years earlier by the Royal Society in London, and which would pass to France when the Encyclopédie began appearing, was held by Scotland in just those years when Jefferson was laying his own intellectual foundation, under the guidance of a typical product of the Scottish efflorescence, William Small. By 1781, when Jefferson was composing his *Notes on the State of Virginia,* he could say that Great Britain's empire was "fast descending" because "her philosophy has crossed the channel, her freedom the Atlantic" (65). The philosophy he speaks of was that of the great Scottish thinkers of the midcentury. For him Scotland was a country "possessing science in as high a degree as any place in the world" (*Papers,* 9:59–60).

America in general had gone to school to the Scots in its last colonial period. At Princeton, Dr. Witherspoon was teaching his Presbyterian students (including his future son-in-law Samuel Stanhope Smith), and even an odd Anglican outsider like James Madison, from the ethics texts of Francis Hutcheson. At the College of Philadelphia, that tempestuous Scot William Smith aimed his curriculum toward the culminating study of the same philosopher, and Francis Alison drilled five future signers of the Declaration of Independence in Hutcheson's texts (cf. D. F. Norton, *Studies on Voltaire,* vol. 154, 1976). Even at the established church's King's College in New York, the moral philosophy of Hutcheson, a dissenting minister, took up the final two years of study. (See Anna Haddow's *Political Science in American Colleges,* 11–12, 14 and Douglas Sloan's *The Scottish Enlightenment and the American College Ideal,* 76, 122–25). Benjamin Franklin's scientific ties with Scotland were very close, as were those of men like Ezra Stiles (Sloan, 1–2, 86–88).

What was true of America in general had particular import for Virginia, where a Scot educated at Marischal College in Aberdeen had founded the College of William and Mary in the seventeenth century. A wave of Scottish Presbyterian emigrants, washed up toward and past the Piedmont of Jefferson's home, was cresting during Jefferson's youth. Lord Bute had made the Scots prominent in colonial administration — nowhere more so than in Virginia, which had a Sottish governor (Robert Dinwiddie) during the 1750s. There was a regular exchange of people and goods between Scotland and Virginia, since Glasgow was the principal port for receiving the colony's tobacco (cf. J. A. Price, *William & Mary Quarterly,* 1954). Jefferson himself

had a regular agent for purchasing books and other things in Glasgow—
Alexander McCaul, a Scot who had spent time on business in Virginia (*Papers*, 1:97, 51–52, 92–93). A wave of young teachers and ministers was shaking up the colony, to the distress of conservatives like Edmund Pendleton. Their support helped break the hold of the religious establishment, paving the way for Jefferson's statute of religious toleration. (Jefferson's own principal teacher at William and Mary, William Small, tried to have the oath of allegiance set aside as a requirement for the presidency of that college.)

Even the Anglican parson who first taught Jefferson his letters (Greek, Latin, and French) was a Scot, William Douglas of Glencairn, who had been trained at Glasgow (just before Hutcheson's arrival) and Edinburgh (in "physics" as well as Hebrew). Douglas, who directed Jefferson's studies for four years, had left Scotland in the 1730s—too early to experience the heady ferment just making itself evident at his two colleges. But William Small, a far more talented man, came along at just the right time. Born in 1734, the brother of a brilliant mathematician, Small attended Marischal College during the early fifties. His classmate there was James Macpherson the fabricator of Jefferson's favorite poet, "Ossian." Small studied medicine with John Gregory, the center of a "philosophical" circle in Aberdeen (where he sometimes lectured at King's College). Gregory was the author of an influential work on the animal basis of human education, and his *Father's Legacy* would later be part of Jefferson's library.

Small came to Virginia in 1758, to teach mathematics at the College of William and Mary. Two years later, when Small was twenty-six, Jefferson (ten years his junior) took up residence at the College. Luckily for both men, the demoralized and half-soused faculty chose this moment to fall apart, and young Small became professor of practically everything during Jefferson's years as an undergraduate. In teaching ethical philosophy, Small used the vernacular lecture-course method with which Hutcheson had revitalized teaching in Scotland twenty-five years earlier. Men like Hutcheson and Adam Smith used the ethics course to expound their central philosophical tenets, connecting them with the sciences through mathematics and with "rhetoric" through a philosophy of beauty. Behind it all lay "the moral sense," expounded as an epistemological tool. This seems to be what Small attempted in what Jefferson calls his "regular [i.e., connected] lectures on Ethics, Rhetoric, and Belles Lettres" (Ford, 1:3).

Small, despite great personal charm, ran into enmity at Williamsburg, prompted in part by the popularity of his teaching methods. It came as a relief to everyone but his students when he returned to England for a rest in 1764—his health was never good. He negotiated his return from afar, wondering if the oath of allegiance could be set aside to make him president of the college. In 1767 he undertook to select the "philosophical apparatus" (i.e., laboratory equipment) for the college; his well-chosen instruments became the possession of Rev. James Madison, with whom Jefferson would conduct his meteorological experiments through the years.

Before Small left Williamsburg, he had included Jefferson in a friendship with the two older men in Williamsburg who were most alive to the intellectual forces of their time — Governor Francis Fauquier, a member of the Royal Society who had been connected with that center of scientific interest, the Royal Mint; and the self-educated classicist and lawyer, George Wythe, who (as we have seen) alone stood by Jefferson's "moral sense" defense of the Revolution as based on the right of expatriation.

Back in Scotland, Small picked up his physician's degree at Marischal College (based on his earlier studies there with Dr. Gregory) and went to London. There he was processed through that great intellectual control center, Benjamin Franklin, who circuited him off to Matthew Boulton in Birmingham. Boulton was a principal Maecenas of the early industrial revolution; and Small, with his genius for friendship, became the great dispenser of amity at the Soho estate Boulton called his "*hôtel de l'amitié.*" Around Boulton and Small and Erasmus Darwin gathered a band of jesting experimenters who became known as the Lunar Society, the butt of Blake's satire, *An Island in the Moon.* The Lunar Society came, in time, to include James Watt and Joseph Priestly and Josiah Wedgwood.

Though Small was a physician optimistic on principle, he was cursed with bad health and fits of depression. When the hypochondriac James Watt stopped off in Birmingham on his way back from London to Glasgow, the two Scots of similar temper became instant friends and began a long correspondence. Small was Watt's intermediary when Watt sought new backing (from Boulton) for his steam "fire engine." The two men bantered and badgered each other into intermittent cheerfulness, joking about death and sex while trading notes on their inventions.

For Small was a creative "mechanic" in the *médecin-philosophe* tradition of his time. He took out patents on new kinds of clocks — one hydraulically driven, one without hands. It is easy to see why Jefferson, with his hero worship for Rittenhouse, admired his own teacher, who could design a "clock with one wheel of nine inches diameter which is to tell hours, minutes, and seconds, and strike, and repeat, and be made for thirty shillings" (Dickinson and Jenkins, *James Watt and the Steam Engine,* 31–35). Small and Watt debated the concept of a "spiral oar" nearly half a century before the screw propellor was made to work. Small would be famous in the history of science if he had lived a few years longer: his name was scheduled to join Watt's and Boulton's in the firm producing steam engines. But the poor health Small tried to drug and jest away from Watt felled Small himself at the early age of forty-one. The year was 1775, and his former student in America had just sent him three dozen bottles of Madeira — grateful, despite the war already begun with Great Britain and its "Scotch mercenaries," to the man who had opened up for him "the system of things in which we are placed."

Jefferson spent the four most intellectually exciting and influential years of his life studying that entire "system of things" under Small's guidance. Then he stayed on in Williamsburg for three more years, reading and trading ideas with the two friends to whom Small had introduced him. (Jefferson's best young friend at Williamsburg, John Page of nearby Rosewell, was also an admiring student of Small. When Jefferson and Page studied their astronomy in the lofty lantern-cupolas of Rosewell, they were continuing work first done under Small's instruction.)

The ideas expressed by Jefferson in 1776 were first introduced to him, and examined by him, in the prior decade of intense reading and discussion that formed his mind. These same ideas went into his major philosophical work, the *Notes on the State of Virginia,* composed five years after the Declaration, when Jefferson had still made only a few short journeys outside of Virginia. Those ideas were not derived, primarily, from Philadelphia or Paris, but from Aberdeen and Edinburgh and Glasgow. We have enough evidence of his reading, and of his conclusions from that reading, to establish that the real lost world of Thomas Jefferson was the world of William Small, the invigorating realm of the Scottish Enlightenment at its zenith.

Note

1. Becker makes only one attempt to trace a verbal echo, at second hand through James Wilson. . . . Chinard found more parallels in Montesquieu than in Locke (*Commonplace Book,* 258–61).

Bibliography

Becker, Carl L. *The Declaration of Independence: A Study in the History of Political Ideas.* New York: Harcourt, Brace, 1922. Reprint, New York: Knopf, 1942.

Boorstin, Daniel. *The Lost World of Thomas Jefferson.* New York: Holt, 1948.

Boyd, Julian P. et al., eds. *The Papers of Thomas Jefferson.* 25 vols. Princeton: Princeton University Press, 1950–.

Cappon, Lester J. *The Adams-Jefferson Letters.* Chapel Hill: University of North Carolina Press, 1959.

Chinard, Gilbert. *Jefferson et les Idéologues: D'après sa Correspondance Inédits avec Destutt de Tracy, Cabnis, J. B. Say, et Auguste Comte.* Baltimore: Johns Hopkins University Press, 1925.

———, ed. *The Commonplace Book of Thomas Jefferson.* Baltimore: Johns Hopkins University Press, 1926.

Dickinson, H. W., and Rhys Jenkins. *James Watt and the Steam Engine: The Memorial Vol-*

ume Prepared for the Committee of the Watt Centenary Commemoration at Birming-ham, 1919. Ashbourne, Derbyshire, England: Moorland, 1981.

Dunn, John. "The Politics of John Locke in England and America in the Eighteenth Century." In *John Locke: Problems and Perspectives: A Collection of New Essays.* Edited by John W. Yolton. London: Cambridge University Press, 1969.

Ford, Paul Leicester, ed. *The Writings of Thomas Jefferson.* 10 vols. New York: Putnam's, 1892–99.

Haddow, Anna. *Political Science in American Colleges and Universities, 1636–1900.* New York: Octagon Books, 1969.

Jefferson, Thomas. *Notes on the State of Virginia.* New York: Norton, 1972.

Koch, Adrienne. *The Philosophy of Thomas Jefferson.* New York: Columbia University Press, 1943.

Lipscomb, A. A., and A. E. Bergh. *The Writings of Thomas Jefferson.* 20 vols. Washington, D.C.: Thomas Jefferson Memorial Association of the United States, 1903.

Peden, William. *Some Aspects of Jeffersonian Bibliography: A Paper Read before the Bibliographical Society of America.* Lexington, Va.: Journalism Laboratory Press, Washington and Lee University, 1941.

Peterson, Merrill D. *The Jefferson Image in the American Mind.* New York: Oxford University Press, 1960.

Robbins, Caroline. *The Eighteenth-Century Commonwealthman.* Cambridge, Mass.: Harvard University Press, 1959.

Sloan, Douglas. *The Scottish Enlightenment and the American College Ideal.* New York: Teachers College Press, Columbia University, 1971.

Sowerby, E. Millicent, comp. *Catalog of the Library of Thomas Jefferson.* 5 vols. Washington, D.C.: Library of Congress, 1953.

Wilson, Douglas L., ed. *Jefferson's Literary Commonplace Book.* Princeton: Princeton University Press, 1989.

4. What was the cast of Jefferson's mind?

Joseph J. Ellis

The Spring of '76: Texts and Contexts

From *American Sphinx: The Character of Thomas Jefferson*

If the mythical view of the Declaration suggests that its words appeared to Jefferson by means of divine inspirations, and the scholarly view has focused on the books which may have influenced him, the selection by Joseph J. Ellis argues that the most formative force was the cast of Jefferson's own mind. To be sure, Ellis believes that the literary influences on Jefferson — the proverbial battle of the books — are important to know. But writing in the wake of the debate between Becker and Wills, he emphasizes the highly moralistic and melodramatic framework that Jefferson imposed on what he read. The result is an interpretation that makes the Declaration a more radical and idealist document driven by Jefferson's sincere vision of a wholly corrupt British government and an equally pure and innocent America. What other members of the Continental Congress considered propaganda, Jefferson regarded as an accurate description of the eternal clash between good and evil.

Questions for a Closer Reading

1. Why does Ellis characterize Jefferson's mode of thinking as "youthful"?

2. According to Ellis, what are the main components of Jefferson's ideal world?

3. Ellis gives most of the credit for drafting the Declaration to Jefferson, but states that Jefferson was given the task

because "the other eligible authors had more important things to do." How does this assertion color the myths surrounding the Declaration's authorship?

4. Ellis notes Jefferson's central role in drafting the Declaration but goes even further, writing "The members of the Continental Congress had placed the ideal instrument in the perfect position at precisely the right moment." Why does Ellis claim in essence that Jefferson was the only man in America who could have produced this document?

5. Why does Ellis set the Declaration against a background of contemporary politics rather than European philosophy?

6. How did Jefferson's own actions and language contribute to the mythical stature of his authorship of the Declaration?

The Spring of '76: Texts and Contexts

[Jefferson sequestered himself at Monticello for the entire winter of 1776.]

He arrived back in Philadelphia on May 14. Not only did he lack any inkling of the historic events that were about to transpire — he confessed that he was completely out of touch with the evolving situation in Congress — but he even tried to persuade friends in Virginia to have him recalled. The Virginia legislature was meeting in convention at Williamsburg to draft a state constitution, and Jefferson, like a good many other delegates in Philadelphia, presumed that the most crucial political business was now occurring at the state rather than national level. The act of drafting new state constitutions, he noted, "is the whole object of the present controversy." He meant that the establishment of state governments was the most discernible way to declare American independence, indicating as it did the

Joseph J. Ellis, *American Sphinx: The Character of Thomas Jefferson* (New York: Knopf, 1997), 46–59.

assumption of political responsibility for the management of American domestic affairs. (John Adams agreed with this perspective and, leaving nothing to chance, had spent the spring designing model constitutions for several states.) Peyton Randolph, Edmund Pendleton, and Patrick Henry all had opted to remain back home in the Old Dominion, either to oversee the drafting of Virginia's constitution or to take the field against Dunmore's ragtag army of former slaves and loyalists. George Washington was in the field organizing the Continental Army. Philadelphia, or so it seemed, had become a mere sideshow.[1]

But Philadelphia was where duty demanded that Jefferson place himself. Anticipating the imminent arrival of a hot and humid summer, he decided to shift his lodgings to the outskirts of the city in order to "have the benefits of a freely circulating air." On May 23 he moved his Windsor chair and writing desk into new quarters on the second floor of a three-story brick house at the corner of Market and Seventh streets. The chair, the desk and the entire dwelling were about to become sacred relics of what history was to record as America's most miraculous moment.[2]

During the next six weeks, from mid-May to early July 1776, Jefferson wrote the words that made him famous and that, over the course of the next two centuries, associated him with the most visionary version of the American dream. As a result, this historical ground has been trampled over by hordes of historians, and the air surrounding it is perpetually full of an incandescent mixture of incense and smoke. His authorship of the Declaration of Independence is regarded as one of those few quasi-religious episodes in American history, that moment when, at least according to the most romantic explanations, a solitary Jefferson was allowed a glimpse of the eternal truths and then offered the literary inspiration to inscribe them on the American soul.

Given this supercharged context, it is the beginning of all genuine wisdom to recognize that neither Jefferson nor any other of the participants foresaw the historical significance of what they were doing at the time. What's more, within the context of Philadelphia in the summer of 1776, the writing of the Declaration of Independence did not seem nearly so important as other priorities, including the constitution-making of the states and the prospect of foreign alliances with France or Spain. The golden haze around the Declaration had not yet formed. The sense of history we bring to the subject did not exist for those making it.

One man, John Adams, has left a record that suggests he *was* conscious of being "present at the creation." In May he wrote to his beloved Abigail in a prophetic mood: "When I consider the great Events which are passed, and those greater which are rapidly advancing, and that I may have been instrumental in touching some Springs, and turning some small Wheels, which have had and will have such Effects, I feel an Awe upon my Mind, which is not easily described." Two weeks later he announced to Abigail that he had begun to make copies of all his letters, a clear sign that he was sending them to posterity. But Adams was hardly typical. His neurotic sensitivity to his own place in history became legendary. And his remarks at the time referred to actions in the Continental Congress requiring the states to draft new constitutions, not to the drafting of the Declaration, which he considered a merely ornamental afterthought.[3]

Jefferson, for his part, remained focused on events back in Virginia. Throughout the weeks of late May and early June he devoted the bulk of his energies to producing three different drafts of a new constitution for his home state. Clearly influenced by the John Adams pamphlet *Thoughts on Government,* Jefferson emphasized the separation of powers, an independent judiciary and a bicameral legislature, with a weak executive (called the Administrator in order to signify his lack of governing power). Every political paper that Jefferson had written up to this point in his life had been a protest statement against some aspect of British policy. Therefore it is interesting to note that his initial effort at a positive and practical vision of government recommended a constitutional structure that adopted the general form of the old colonial governments, the exception being the diminution of executive authority, clearly a lesson rooted in the colonial resistance to gubernatorial claims of royal prerogative.[4]

Anyone on the lookout for more avowedly progressive features in Jefferson's thinking could have found them. Although he required a property qualification for all voters, he also proposed a land distribution policy that would provide fifty acres for each resident. He quietly inserted a radical provision for complete religious freedom. And he urged that the new constitution be ratified by a special convention called exclusively for that purpose rather than by the sitting legislature, a democratic idea that John Adams had also proposed as a way of implementing the principle of popular sovereignty. All in all, Jefferson's prescriptions for the new Virginian republic were an impressive blend of traditional forms and selective reforms. They establish the historically correct, if unorthodox, context for answering the proverbial question: What was Jefferson thinking about on the eve of his authorship of the Declaration of Independence? The answer is indisputable. He was not thinking, as some historians have claimed, about John Locke's theory of natural rights or Scottish commonsense philosophy. He was thinking about Virginia's new constitution.[5]

An aspect of his thinking proved directly relevant for the task he was about to assume. In his preamble to the first and third drafts of the Virginia constitution, he composed a bill of indictment against George III. One could see glimmerings of these charges against the British monarch in *Sum-*

mary View, then even more explicit accusations in *Causes and Necessities.* But the lengthy condemnation of the king in his draft constitution extended the list of crimes against colonial rights. It was in effect his penultimate draft for the list of grievances that became the longest section of the Declaration of Independence.

One of the grievances stands out, in part because it dealt with what soon proved to be the most controversial issue during the debate in Congress over the wording of the Declaration, in part because of the difference between what Jefferson wrote for the Virginia constitution in May and what he wrote for the Declaration in June. This is the passage in the Declaration in which Jefferson blamed George III for instigating and perpetuating the slave trade, thereby implying that slavery was an evil institution imposed on the colonists by a corrupt monarch. In the earlier draft for the Virginia constitution, however, he charged George III with "prompting our negroes to rise in arms against us; those very negroes who by an inhuman use of his negative he hath refused us permission to exclude by law." Here one can see Jefferson juggling two incompatible formulations: One is to blame the king for slavery; the other is to blame him for emancipating the slaves (i.e., Lord Dunmore's proclamation). It was symptomatic of a deep disjunction in his thinking about slavery that he never reconciled.[6]

Another one of the proverbial questions — how or why was Jefferson selected to draft the Declaration? — is also answerable with a recovery of the immediate context. The short answer is that he was the obvious choice on the basis of his past work in the Congress as a draftsman. That was his specialty. The longer answer emerges clearly from the situation that existed in the Congress in June 1776.

Virginia had taken the lead by instructing its delegates on May 15 to propose total and complete American independence from Great Britain. On June 7 Richard Henry Lee moved the resolution "that these United Colonies are, and of right ought to be, free and independent States. . . ." A debate then ensued over when the vote on Lee's resolution should occur. The Congress decided to delay a vote until July 1, in deference to delegations that were still divided (i.e., Pennsylvania) and to delegations that lacked clear instructions from their state legislatures (i.e., New York). In the meantime a committee could be working on a document that implemented the Lee resolution. A Virginian presence on the committee was essential, and Jefferson was the most appropriate Virginian, both because of his reputation as a writer and because Lee, the other possible choice, was the author of the resolution before the Congress and presumably would lead the debate in its behalf.[7]

The committee convened shortly after it was appointed on June 11. (Besides Adams and Jefferson, it included Benjamin Franklin, Robert Livingston and Roger Sherman.) The rest of the committee delegated the drafting to Adams and Jefferson. At this point one can reasonably ask why Adams did not write it himself. This was a question Adams raised with himself countless times over the ensuing years, as the significance of the Declaration grew in the popular imagination and Jefferson's authorship became his major ticket into the American pantheon. In his autobiography Adams recalled that he delegated the task to Jefferson for several reasons, among them his sense that his own prominence as a leader of the radical faction in Congress for the past two years would subject the draft to greater scrutiny and criticism. But such latter-day recollections only tend to obscure the more elemental fact that no one at the time regarded the drafting of the Declaration as a major responsibility or honor. Adams, like Lee, would be needed to lead the debate on the floor. That was considered the crucial arena. Jefferson was asked to draft the Declaration of Independence, then, in great part because the other eligible authors had more important things to do.[8]

Context is absolutely crucial. For all intents and purposes, the decision to declare independence had already been made. Thomas Paine's *Common Sense,* published in January, had swept through the colonies like a firestorm, destroying any final vestige of loyalty to the British crown. In May the Congress had charged each colony to draft new state constitutions, an explicit act of political independence that Adams always regarded as the decisive move. Most important, the war itself had been raging for more than a year. The bulk of the Congress's time in fact was occupied with wartime planning and military decisions, as the British fleet was sighted off the coasts of New York and South Carolina and an American expeditionary force to Canada met with humiliating defeat. (One more debacle or major military blunder, and the American war for independence might have been over before the delegates in Philadelphia got around to declaring it started.) Nothing about the scene permitted much confidence or the opportunity to be contemplative. It did not seem to be a propitious moment for literary craftsmanship.

But whether they knew it or not — and there was no earthly way they could have known — the members of the Continental Congress had placed the ideal instrument in the perfect position at precisely the right moment. Throughout the remainder of his long career Jefferson never again experienced a challenge better suited to call forth his best creative energies. The work had to be done alone, isolated from the public debates. It needed to possess an elevated quality that linked American independence to grand and great forces that transcended the immediate political crisis and swept the imagination upward toward a purer and more principled world. Finally, it needed to paint the scene in bright, contrasting colors of truth and falsehood, right and wrong, "ought" and "is" without any of the intermediate hues or lingering doubts. It is difficult to imagine anyone in America better equipped, by disposition and experience, to perform the task as well.

Jefferson wrote the Declaration of Independence in a matter of a few days — Adams later remembered it took him only "a day or two" — and then showed the draft to Adams and Franklin, later recalling that "they were the two members of whose judgments and amendments I wished most to have the benefit." They suggested a few minor revisions (i.e., replacing "sacred & undeniable truths" with "self-evident truths"); then the committee placed the document before the Continental Congress on June 28. After Lee's resolution was debated and passed (July 1–2), the Congress took up the wording of the Declaration; it made several major changes and excised about one-quarter of the text. During the debate Jefferson sat silently and sullenly, regarding each proposed revision as another defacement. Franklin sat next to him and tried to soothe his obvious pain with the story of a sign painter commissioned by a hatter, who kept requesting more concise language for his sign until nothing was left on the sign but a picture of a hat. On July 4 the Congress approved its revised version and the Declaration of Independence was sent to the printer for publication. Jefferson later recalled that it was signed by the members of Congress on that day, but that is almost surely not correct. The parchment copy was signed by most members on August 2.[9]

Most of the debate in the Congress and most of the revisions of Jefferson's draft of the Declaration focused on the long bill of indictment against George III, the section that modern readers care about least. When Jefferson much later insisted that he was not striving for "originality of principle or sentiment" but was seeking only to provide an "expression of the American mind," he was probably referring to this section, which was intended to sum up the past twelve years of colonial opposition to British policy in language designed to make the king responsible for all the trouble. Jefferson had been practicing this list of grievances for more than two years, first in *Summary View,* then in *Causes and Necessity* and then in his drafts of the Virginia constitution. "I expected you had . . . exhausted the Subject of Complaint against Geo. 3d. and was at a loss to discover what the Congress would do for one to their Declaration of Independence without copying," wrote Edmund Pendleton when he first saw the official version, "but find that you have acquitted yourselves very well on that score."[10]

As an elegant, if decidedly one-sided, version of recent Anglo-American history, this section of the Declaration has certainly stood the test of time, providing students of the American Revolution with a concise summary of the constitutional crisis from the colonists' perspective at the propitious moment. As a reflection of Jefferson's thinking, however, it is missing three distinctive and distinctively Jeffersonian perspectives on the conflict. When Jefferson wrote back to friends in Virginia, complaining that critics in the Congress had, as one friend put it, "mangled . . . the Manuscript," these were the three major revisions he most regretted.[11]

First, as we noticed earlier, the Congress deleted the long passage blaming George III for waging "cruel war against human nature itself" by establishing slavery in North America; Jefferson also accused the king of blocking colonial efforts to end the slave trade, then "exciting those very people to rise in arms against us . . . by murdering the people on whom he has also obtruded them." Several complicated and even tortured ideas are struggling for supremacy here. One can surmise that the members of Congress decided to delete it out of sheer bewilderment, since the passage mixes together an implicit moral condemnation of slavery with an explicit condemnation of the British monarch for both starting it and trying to end it.

In his own notes on the debate in Congress Jefferson claimed that the opposition was wholly political. Several southern delegations, especially those of South Carolina and Georgia, opposed any restraint on the importation of slaves, he reported, adding that their "Northern brethren also I believe felt a little tender under those censures; for tho' their people have very few slaves themselves, yet they had been pretty considerable carriers of them to others." Jefferson's clear implication is that he was trying to take a principled stand against both slavery and the slave trade but that a majority of delegates were unprepared to go along with him.[12]

The truth was much messier. With regard to the trade, Jefferson knew from his experience in the House of Burgesses that many established slaveowners in the Tidewater region favored an end of imports because their own plantations were already well stocked and new arrivals only reduced the value of their own slave population. Ending the trade in Virginia, in short, was not at all synonymous with ending slavery. With regard to slavery itself, Jefferson's formulation made great polemic sense but historical and intellectual nonsense. It absolved slaveowners like himself from any responsibility or complicity in the establishment of an institution that was clearly at odds with the values on which the newly independent America was based. Slavery was another one of those vestiges of feudalism foisted upon the liberty-loving colonists by the evil heir to the Norman Conquest. This was complete fiction, of course, but also completely in accord with Jefferson's urge to preserve the purity of his moral dichotomies and his romantic view of America's uncontaminated origins. Slavery was the serpent in the garden sent there by a satanic king. But the moral message conveyed by this depiction was not emancipation so much as commiseration. Since the colonists had nothing to do with establishing slavery — they were the unfortunate victims of English barbarism — they could not be blamed for its continuance. This was less a clarion call to end slavery than an invitation to wash one's hands of the matter.[13]

Second, Jefferson tried once again, as he had tried before in *Causes and Necessity,* to insert his favorite theory of expatriation, claiming that the first settlers came over at their own expense and initiative "unassisted by the wealth or the strength of Great Britain." His obsessive insistence on this theme derived from his devotion to the Saxon myth,* which allowed for the neat separation of Whiggish colonists and feudal or absolutist English ministers. The tangled history of imperial relations did not fit very well into these political categories, but Jefferson found it much easier to revise the history (i.e., claiming there had never been any colonial recognition of royal or parliamentary authority) than give up his moral dichotomies. Once again his colleagues in the Continental Congress found his argument excessive.[14]

Third, the last excision came toward the very end of Jefferson's draft. It was a rousingly emotional passage with decidedly sentimental overtones that condemned "our British brethren" for sending over "not only souldiers of our common blood, but Scotch & foreign mercenaries to invade and destroy us." It went on: "These facts have given the last stab to agonizing affection, and manly spirit bids us to renounce for ever these unfeeling brethren. We must endeavor to forget our former love for them, and to hold them as we hold the rest of mankind, enemies in war, in peace friends; but a communication of grandeur & of freedom it seems is below their dignity. Be it so, since they will have it. The road to happiness & to glory is open to us too. We will tread it apart from them. . . ." This was a remarkable piece of rhetoric that Jefferson apparently regarded as one of his better creations. Even at the end of his life he was bitter about its deletion. "The pusillanimous idea that we had friends in England worth keeping terms with, still haunted the minds of many," he recalled, and therefore "those passages which conveyed censures on the people of England were struck out, lest they should give them offence."[15]

What strikes the modern reader is not the timidity of the Continental Congress for excising the passage so much as the melodramatic sentimentalism of Jefferson in composing it. As with the expatriation theory, Jefferson was anxious to depict the separation of the colonies from the British Empire as a decision forced upon the colonists, who are passive victims rather than active agents of revolution. But here the broken bonds are more affective than political. A relationship based on love and trust has been violated, and the betrayed partner, the colonists, is bravely moving forward in life, wounded by the rejection but ready to face alone a glorious future that might otherwise have been shared together. This is a highly idealized and starkly sentimental rendering of how and why emotional separations happen, a projection onto the imperial crisis of the romantic innocence Jefferson had displayed in his adolescent encounters with young women, an

---

*saxon myth: The belief that the pure Saxon values of early England were corrupted by the Norman invaders of 1066, who imposed feudalism on the country.

all-or-nothing-at-all mentality that the other delegates found inappropriate for a state paper purporting to convey more sense than sensibility.

The most famous section of the Declaration, which has become the most quoted statement of human rights in recorded history as well as the most eloquent justification of revolution on behalf of them, went through the Continental Congress without comment and with only one very minor change. These are, in all probability, the best-known fifty-eight words in American history: "We hold these truths to be self evident; that all men are created equal; that they are endowed by their Creator with certain [inherent and] inalienable Rights; that among these are life, liberty & the pursuit of happiness; that to secure these rights, governments are instituted among men, deriving their just powers from the consent of the governed." This is the seminal statement of the American Creed, the closest approximation to political poetry ever produced in American culture. In the nineteenth century Abraham Lincoln, who also knew how to change history with words, articulated with characteristic eloquence the quasi-religious view of Jefferson as the original American oracle: "All honor to Jefferson — to the man who, in the concrete pressure of a struggle for national independence by a single people, had the coolness, forecaste, and capacity to introduce into a merely revolutionary document, an abstract truth, and so to embalm it there, that today and in all coming days, it shall be a rebuke and a stumbling block to the very harbingers of reappearing tyranny and oppression." The entire history of liberal reform in America can be written as a process of discovery, within Jefferson's words, of a spiritually sanctioned mandate for ending slavery, providing the rights of citizenship to blacks and women, justifying welfare programs for the poor and expanding individual freedoms.[16]

No serious student of either Jefferson or the Declaration of Independence has ever claimed that he foresaw all or even most of the ideological consequences of what he wrote. But the effort to explain what *was* in his head has spawned almost as many interpretations as the words themselves have generated political movements. Jefferson himself was accused of plagiarism by enemies or jealous friends on so many occasions throughout his career that he developed a standard reply. "Neither aiming at originality of principle or sentiment, nor yet copied from any particular and previous writing," he explained, he drew his ideas from "the harmonizing sentiments of the day, whether expressed in letters, printed essays or in the elementary books of public right, as Aristotle, Cicero, Locke, Sidney, etc."[17]

This is an ingeniously double-edged explanation, for it simultaneously disavows any claims to originality and yet insists that he depended upon no specific texts or sources. The image it conjures up is that of a medium, sitting alone at the writing desk and making himself into an instrument for the accumulated wisdom and "harmonizing sentiments" of the ages. It is only a short step from this image to Lincoln's vision of Jefferson as oracle or prophet, receiving the message from the gods and sending it on to us and then to the ages. Given the creedal character of the natural rights section of the Declaration, several generations of American interpreters have felt the irresistible impulse to bathe the scene in speckled light and cloudy mist, thereby implying that efforts to dispel the veil of mystery represent some vague combination of sacrilege and treason.

Any serious attempt to pierce through this veil must begin by recovering the specific conditions inside that room on Market and Seventh streets in June 1776. Even if we take Jefferson at his word, that he did not copy sections of the Declaration from any particular books, he almost surely had with him copies of his own previous writings, to include *Summary View, Causes and Necessity* and his three drafts of the Virginia constitution. This is not to accuse him of plagiarism, unless one wishes to argue that an author can plagiarize himself. It is to say that virtually all the ideas found in the Declaration and much of the specific language, especially the grievances against George III, had already found expression in those earlier writings.

Recall the context. The Congress is being overwhelmed with military reports of imminent American defeat in New York and Canada. The full Congress is in session six days a week, and committees are meeting throughout the evenings. The obvious practical course for Jefferson to take was to rework his previous drafts on the same general theme. While it seems almost sacrilegious to suggest that the creative process that produced the Declaration was a cut-and-paste job, it strains credulity and common sense to the breaking point to believe that Jefferson did not have these items at his elbow and draw liberally from them when drafting the Declaration.

His obvious preoccupation with the ongoing events at the Virginia convention, which was drafting the Virginia constitution at just this time, is also crucial to remember. Throughout late May and early June couriers moved back and forth between Williamsburg and Philadelphia, carrying Jefferson's drafts for a new constitution to the convention and reports on the debate there to the Continental Congress. On June 12 the Virginians unanimously adopted a preamble drafted by George Mason that contained these words: "All men are created equally free and independent and have certain inherent and natural rights . . . , among which are the enjoyment of life and liberty, with the means of acquiring and possessing property, and pursuing and obtaining happiness and safety." The *Pennsylvania Gazette* published Mason's words the same day they were adopted in Williamsburg. Since Jefferson's version of the same thought was drafted sometime that following week, and since we know that he regarded the unfolding events in Virginia as more significant than what was occurring in Philadelphia and that he was being kept abreast by courier, it also strains credulity to deny the influence of Mason's language on his own.[18]

While that explains the felicitous phrase "pursuit of happiness," which Mason himself could have picked up from several English and American sources, it does not explain Jefferson's much-debated deletion of "property," the conventional third right memorialized in Locke's *Second Treatise on Government*. He made that choice on his own. He was probably aware that Mason's language had generated spirited opposition from a segment of the planter class in Virginia who worried that it implied a repudiation of slavery; they insisted on an amendment that excluded slaves by adding the qualifying clause "when they enter into a state of society." All this suggests that Jefferson was probably aware of the contradiction between his own version of the natural rights philosophy and the institution of slavery. By dropping any reference to "property" he blurred that contradiction. This helps answer the intriguing question of why no debate over the issue occurred in the Continental Congress, as it did in the Virginia convention. Perhaps the debate over the slave trade provision also served that purpose.[19]

Beyond the question of immediate influences on Jefferson's choice of words and his way of framing the case for independence, however, lies the more murky question of the long-term influences on his political thinking. Granted that his own earlier writings and drafts of the Virginia constitution almost certainly lay strewn across his lap and writing desk, where did the ideas contained in those documents come from? Granted that we know beyond a reasonable doubt what Jefferson was looking at, that he and the other delegates in the Congress were under enormous pressure to manage the ongoing war as military disaster loomed in Canada and New York, so he had little time to do more than recycle his previous writings, what core of ideas was already fixed in his head?

The available answers fall into two primary headings, each argued persuasively by prominent scholars and each finding the seminal source of Jefferson's political thought in particular books. The older and still more venerable interpretation locates the intellectual wellspring in John Locke. Even during Jefferson's lifetime several commentators, usually intending to question his originality, noted that the doctrine of natural rights and the corollary endorsement of rightful revolution came straight out of Locke's *Second Treatise*. Richard Henry Lee, for example, claimed that Jefferson had merely "copied from Locke's treatise on government." Several conclusions followed naturally from the Lockean premise, the chief ones being that Jeffersonian thought was inherently liberal and individualistic and, despite the substitution of "pursuit of happiness" for "property," fundamentally compatible with America's emerging capitalistic mentality.[20]

The second and more recent interpretive tradition locates the source of Jefferson's thinking in the Scottish Enlightenment, especially the moral philosophy of Francis Hutcheson. The key insight here is that Jefferson's belief in the natural equality of man derived primarily from Hutcheson's doctrine of the "moral sense," a faculty inherent in all human beings that no mere government could violate. Moreover, the Scottish school of thought linked Jefferson to a more communal or collectivistic tradition that was at odds with Lockean liberalism and therefore incompatible with unbridled individualism, especially the sort of individualism associated with predatory behavior in the marketplace.[21]

There is, in fact, a third most recent and most novel interpretation, at once brilliant and bizarre, that operates from the premise that Jefferson intended the Declaration to be read aloud or performed. This claim is based on the discovery that his final draft was punctuated by a series of quotation marks designed to guide the reading of the document in order to enhance its dramatic effect. This discovery has led to the conclusion that Jefferson was influenced by the new books on rhetoric by such English authors as James Burgh and Thomas Sheridan, in which spoken language was thought to derive its power by playing on the unconscious emotions of the audience. The secret power of the Declaration, so this argument goes, derives from Jefferson's self-conscious orchestration of language, informed by the new rhetoric, which overrides all contradictions (i.e., slavery and human equality; individualism and community) in a kind of verbal symphony that still plays on within American political culture.[22]

Each of these interpretations offers valuable insights into the intellectual sources of Jefferson's thinking as he sat down to write the Declaration. Clearly, he knew his Locke, though his favorite Lockean treatise was not the one on government but the *Essay on Human Understanding*. That said, the fundamental claim that revolution is justified if the existent rulers demonstrate systematic disregard for the rights of their subjects certainly originated with Locke. Jefferson may have gotten his specific language from George Mason, but both men knew whom they were paraphrasing. Just as clearly, Jefferson believed that the distinguishing feature that made human beings fully human, and in that sense equal, was the moral sense. Whether he developed that belief by reading Hutcheson or any of the other members of the Scottish school or from his own personal observation of human behavior is ultimately unknowable and not terribly important.

The claim that Jefferson meant the Declaration to be read aloud is more difficult to swallow. A simpler explanation of his unusual punctuation marks would be that he was worried that he might be required to read the document aloud when the committee presented it to the Congress on June 28, so he inserted oratorical guides for his delivery, not trusting his own famously inadequate speaking ability. (We really don't know whether he himself read it or whether it was read by the secretary of the Congress.) But the recognition that the Declaration plays on the sentiments of readers and listeners, that its underlying tones and rhythms operate in mysterious ways to win assent despite logical contradictions and disjunctions, is a key insight very much worth pondering.

The central problem with all these explanations, however, is that they make Jefferson's thinking an exclusive function of books. True, he read voraciously as a young man, took notes on his reading, and left a comprehensive list of the books in his library. Since we know so much about his reading habits, and so little about other aspects of his early life (the Shadwell fire, again), the temptation to make an implicit connection between his ideas and his books is irresistible. Then once the connection is made with, say, Locke or Hutcheson, one can conveniently talk about particular texts as if one were talking about Jefferson's mind. This is a long-standing scholarly tradition — one might call it the scholarly version of poetic license — that depends on the unspoken assumption that what one thinks is largely or entirely a product of what one reads.[23]

In Jefferson's case, it is a very questionable assumption. In the specific case of the natural rights section of the Declaration, it sends us baying down literary trails after false scents of English or Scottish authors, while the object of the hunt sits squarely before us. In all his previous publications the young Thomas Jefferson had demonstrated a strong affinity for and deep attachment to visions of the ideal society. He found it in various locations "back there" in the past: the forests of Saxony; England before the Norman Conquest; the American colonies before the French and Indian War. (Here his previous reading clearly *did* have a discernible influence, though the relevant books were the Whig histories and the Real Whig writings, but they had been so thoroughly digested that their themes and categories blended imperceptibly into Jefferson's cast of mind.) His several arguments for American independence all were shaped around a central motif, in which the imperfect and inadequate present was contrasted with a perfect and pure future, achievable once the sources of corruption were eliminated. His mind instinctively created dichotomies and derived its moral energy from juxtaposing the privileged side of any case or cause with the contaminated side. While his language was often colorful, the underlying message was nearly always painted in black and white.

The vision he projected in the natural rights section of the Declaration, then, represented yet another formulation of the Jeffersonian imagination. The specific form of the vision undoubtedly drew upon language Locke had used to describe the putative conditions of society before governments were established. But the urge to embrace such an ideal society came from deep inside Jefferson himself. It was the vision of a young man projecting his personal cravings for a world in which all behavior was voluntary and therefore all coercion unnecessary, where independence and equality never collided, where the sources of all authority were invisible because they had already been internalized. Efforts on the part of scholars to determine whether Jefferson's prescriptive society was fundamentally individualistic or communal can never reach closure, because within the Jeffersonian utopia such choices do not need to be made. They reconcile themselves naturally.

Though indebted to Locke, Jefferson's political vision was more radical than liberal, driven as it was by a youthful romanticism unwilling to negotiate its high standards with an imperfect world. One of the reasons why European commentators on American politics have found American expectations so excessive and American political thinking in general so beguilingly innocent is that Jefferson provided a sanction for youthful hopes and illusions, planted squarely in what turned out to be the founding document of the American republic. The American dream, then, is just that, the Jeffersonian dream writ large.

Notes

1. Jefferson to Thomas Nelson, May 16, 1776, Julian P. Boyd et al., eds., *The Papers of Thomas Jefferson* (25 vols., Princeton, 1950–), I, 292.

2. Ibid., I, 216–17; Silvio A. Bedini, *Declaration of Independence Desk: Relic of Revolution* (Washington, D.C., 1981), 4–5. Jefferson eventually gave the desk to his granddaughter Ellen Randolph Coolidge as a wedding present in 1825, predicting that "its imaginary value will increase with the years . . . , as the relics of the Saints are in those of the Church."

3. John Adams to Abigail Adams, March 17, 1776, Lyman Butterfield, ed., *Adams Family Correspondence* (3 vols., Cambridge, Mass., 1963), I, 410; John Adams to Abigail Adams, June 2, 1776, ibid., II, 3.

4. Jefferson's three drafts of the Virginia constitution are reproduced in Boyd, I, 329–65.

5. Ibid., I, 362–63, for the most progressive features in Jefferson's third and final draft.

6. Ibid., I, 357.

7. Ibid., I, 312–14, provides Jefferson's notes on the debate in the Continental Congress. The story told here has several contested features, the chief one being the reasons for selecting Jefferson over Lee. The fullest discussion of the controversy is in Henry S. Randall, *The Life of Thomas Jefferson* (3 vols., New York, 1958), I, 145–62. Dumas Malone's synthesis in *Jefferson and His Time* (6 vols., Boston, 1948–81), I, 217–19, is a model of fairness. Lee's resolution of June 7 is reproduced in Boyd, I, 298–99.

8. Lyman Butterfield, ed., *The Diary and Autobiography of John Adams* (4 vols., Cambridge, Mass., 1961), III, 335–37, offers the classic Adams account, which mixes the truth with his own personal need to show posterity that he, not Jefferson, was in charge. For a discussion of Adams's persistent claim that the Declaration was no more than an elegant ornament to the crucial business in the Continental Congress, see Joseph J. Ellis, *Passionate Sage: The Character and Legacy of John Adams* (New York, 1993), 64–65, 99–100.

9. The two authoritative studies of the chronology and different drafts of the Declaration are: Julian Boyd, *The Declaration of Independence: The Evolution of the Text*

(Princeton, 1945) and John H. Hazelton, *The Declaration of Independence* (New York, 1906). Pauline Maier's forthcoming book, *American Scripture: Making the Declaration of Independence* (New York, 1997), which she graciously allowed me to read in draft form and which helped me in the final stages of my own revisions, will unquestioningly become the new standard work. The Adams recollection is from Butterfield, ed., *Diary and Autobiography,* III, 336. Boyd attempts to hold open the possibility that the signing occurred on July 4, as Jefferson claimed, but the scholarly consensus is that Jefferson's memory was wrong. See Boyd, I, 306–07. For a convenient summary of the many myths about the signing ceremony, see Charles Warren, "Fourth of July Myths," *William and Mary Quarterly* [*WMQ*], II (1945), 242–48.

10. Jefferson's recollections are in Jefferson to James Madison, August 30, 1823, James Morton Smith, ed., *The Republic of Letters: The Correspondence Between Thomas Jefferson and James Madison, 1776–1826* (3 vols., New York, 1995), III, 223; Edmund Pendleton to Jefferson, July 22, 1776, Boyd, 471.

11. Jefferson to Richard Henry Lee, July 8, 1776, Boyd, I, 455–56. Boyd's discussion of the revisions made by the Congress is the standard account, summarized in the long editorial note in ibid., I, 413–17. But Boyd's account sometimes loses sight of the substantive issues at stake in ways that seem unnecessarily tedious. I found the account in Garry Wills, *Inventing America: Jefferson's Declaration of Independence* (New York, 1978), 306–17, most sensible.

12. Boyd, I, 314–15, 426.

13. Wills, *Inventing,* 72–73, provides a nice comparison of what Jefferson wrote in his drafts of the Virginia constitution and in the Declaration. It also provides reactions to this specific grievance by the British press, which did not fail to note the moral contradictions of slaveowners trumpeting liberty.

14. Boyd, I, 426.

15. Ibid., I, 426–27; Paul Leicester Ford, ed., *The Writings of Thomas Jefferson* (10 vols., New York, 1892–99), I, 21.

16. Boyd, I, 423; the most elegant version of the reverential interpretation is by Dumas Malone in *Jefferson,* I, 224–25. The Lincoln quotation, which dates from 1859, is cited in Wills, *Inventing,* xxi.

17. Jefferson to Richard Henry Lee, May 8, 1825, Ford, XVI, 118.

18. On Mason's role in the Virginia convention, see Boyd, I, 335.

19. For a convenient summary of the scholarly debate over the phrase "pursuit of happiness," see Wills, *Inventing,* 240–41. For the debate over Mason's language and its implications for slavery in Virginia, see Richard R. Beeman, *Patrick Henry: A Biography* (New York, 1974), 100–02.

20. The classic statement of this liberal interpretation is Carl Becker, *The Declaration of Independence: A Study in the History of Political Ideas* (New York, 1922).

21. The seminal statement of this republican or collectivistic interpretation is Wills, *Inventing.* For a convincing critique of the Wills argument that also reviews the evidence and implications of the Becker–Wills disagreement, see Ronald Hamowy, "Jefferson and the Scottish Enlightenment: A Critique of Garry Wills's Inventing America . . . ," *WMQ* XXXVI (1979), 503–23.

22. Jay Fliegelman, *Declaring Independence: Jefferson, Natural Language, and the Culture of Performance* (Stanford, 1993). For the enthusiastic scholarly reaction to Fliegelman's novel thesis, see Peter Onuf, "The Scholars' Jefferson," *WMQ,* I, (1993), 683–84.

23. Boyd, I, 78–81, for Jefferson's book list in 1771.

Pauline Maier

Mr. Jefferson and His Editors

From *American Scripture: Making
the Declaration of Independence*

The obsession with Jefferson's role in the drafting of the
Declaration, and with what Jefferson read or what was in his
mind, has caused us to forget the important role of the Continental Congress. History, after all, is seldom the product of
singular characters, most often the result of multiple forces
colliding to create outcomes that defy either control or pre-
diction by individual leaders. Here Pauline Maier reminds
us of two important and incontrovertible facts: First, that
no one at the time regarded Jefferson as the author of the
Declaration (he was merely the draftsman); and second,
the delegates to the Continental Congress gave the document its final shape, revising and excising fully one-quarter
of Jefferson's text. Along the way, Maier also reminds us that
our contemporary fascination with the Declaration as the
primal statement of the American Creed was not shared by
most Americans of that distant day. For them, it was less a
philosophical document about the ideals on which America would be based than an assertion of American political
independence from the British Empire.

Questions for a Closer Reading

1. What were the major changes in the Declaration made by
   the Continental Congress? How can you characterize the
   nature of these changes?

2. How was it possible for a large and unwieldy body like the Committee of the Whole to function as editors with such skill?

3. Why did the Continental Congress make grievances against George III the focus of the document?

4. How did the revisions made by Congress improve on Jefferson's draft? For what reasons, other than pride, did Jefferson feel the original was stronger?

5. What difference does it make to think of Jefferson as the "draftsman" of the Declaration rather than its author?

6. How do the changes made by Congress reflect their sense of the future importance of the Declaration? Do any of their edits make the Declaration more or less palatable to a reader today?

7. The clause on slavery is the longest deletion from Jefferson's original draft. Why did Congress decide to take it out? Does any of its original intent remain? Does its deletion strengthen or weaken the argument against George III?

Mr. Jefferson and His Editors

On July 2, after unanimously affirming that "these United Colonies are, and of right, ought to be, Free and Independent States," the Continental Congress resolved itself into a Committee of the Whole to consider the draft Declaration of Independence submitted by the Committee of Five. At that point the official record of Congress's proceedings falls silent until the Committee of the Whole reported later in the day that it needed more time to complete its work. Congress agreed, took up one small piece of business, then adjourned.[1]

Each of the next two days began much the same, as Congress dispatched

Pauline Maier, *American Scripture: Making the Declaration of Independence* (New York: Knopf, 1997), 143–53.

items of pressing business and routine administrative matters — receiving letters, many of which included information on the military situation, settling accounts, responding as best it could to the breaking crisis. Then, having made what provisions it could for holding off the enemy, Congress set the war temporarily aside and, "agreeable to the order of the day," again "resolved itself into a committee of the whole" to consider what it called the "declaration on independence."[2] Once again the curtain fell, concealing the delegates as they moved through the document, making changes as they went along, leaving no official record of their proceedings beyond its fruit — the Declaration that, reconstituted as the Continental Congress, they finally adopted. Even the private correspondence of delegates is remarkably silent on what the Committee of the Whole did and why. Only Jefferson's notes on Congress's proceedings discuss the subject in any detail, and Jefferson was anything but a dispassionate observer as the Committee of the Whole rewrote or chopped off large sections of his draft, eliminating in the end fully a quarter of his text.

How exactly did the Committee of the Whole execute its editorial work? Did one or two delegates take charge, or did many voices feed into the process? We will never know. If there was only one copy, the handwritten "fair copy" submitted by the Committee of Five, how could the delegates examine the text, propose changes, or even understand the revisions others proposed? To that question, at least, the historian Wilfred J. Ritz provides some answers. Unless its members were "dunderheads," he argues, Congress must have had the committee draft printed, and distributed copies to the delegates. None of those copies seems to have survived, and Congress's journal says nothing about having the draft printed — but then the journal made no pretense of offering a complete record of everything Congress did. Perhaps Congress gathered up all earlier printings and destroyed them once it decided upon the Declaration's final form. In working on the Articles of Confederation later in July, it openly followed a very similar procedure.[3] Ritz's theory makes sense, and allows us to imagine the delegates bent over their texts, marking changes, debating whether to move an adverb, change a word, delete a passage here or insert another there.

That Congress was willing to devote such efforts to the document should have been a cause of satisfaction for Jefferson. The draft Declaration submitted to Congress was, as the New Hampshire delegate Josiah Bartlett put it on July 1, "a pretty good one," unlike the initial draft of the Declaration on Taking Up Arms, which in June 1775 Congress sent back to a reconstituted drafting committee for a thorough reworking. Time was also a factor. Congress needed to announce its adoption of Independence as quickly as possible, and in an appropriate way. In short, the relatively obvious character of changes needed in Jefferson's draft, the urgency of issuing a Declaration, and the immediate importance of that document all suggested that Congress should itself take on the task of editing the text.[4]

Some of its changes were verbal. These are perhaps the most moving testament to the delegates' determination to make the Declaration as good as possible. They left most of the well-worked-over opening paragraphs untouched, except Jefferson's "inherent and inalienable rights" became "certain inalienable rights," which was better. ("Inalienable" seems to have become "unalienable" only later, in the course of printing the document.) At Jefferson's reference to "a long train of abuses and usurpations, begun at a distinguished period & pursuing invariably the same object," the delegates cut out "begun at a distinguished period &," which was meant to emphasize that the King's actions had occurred over a long period of time, and so probably seemed of substantive importance to Jefferson, but the phrase made the sentence cumbersome. The delegates were so attentive to detail that at one point they changed "neglected utterly" to "utterly neglected."

More often, however, the delegates cut back or eliminated the more extreme and untenable assertions in the committee draft. In the statement that necessity forced the Americans to "expunge" their former systems of government, the delegates substituted "alter" for "expunge." There were, after all, some parts of their former governments worth keeping — representative assemblies, for example — so "alter" was more accurate. Where Jefferson had accused the King of "unremitting" injuries, the delegates charged him with "repeated" injuries, which was easier to prove, and then cut out the assertion that there appeared in the King's conduct "no solitary fact to contradict the uniform tenor of the rest." They also crossed out the phrase "for the truth of which we pledge a faith yet unsullied by falsehood" from the end of that paragraph, so it ended simply "to prove this let facts be submitted to a candid world." Did they dislike the tone of that assertion? Did they find it arrogant, or pretentious? Or was the problem that it invited silly quibbling over whether the colonists had ever said anything less than entirely truthful? In any case, the change made the connection between that and the next section of document, and so the Declaration's overall structure, more emphatic, which was all to the good.

What adjustments the committee made in the individual charges against the King were, with one exception, of the same sort. The exception concerned the King's "transporting large armies of foreign mercenaries" to America. There the delegates, reflecting the outrage of their constituents, made Jefferson's denunciation even harsher, describing the act as "scarcely paralleled in the most barbarous ages" and inserting "totally" before Jefferson's statement that it was "unworthy the head of a civilized nation." Everywhere else they moderated Jefferson's claims. Where the draft declaration accused George III of dissolving houses of representatives "repeatedly &

continually," the delegates crossed out "& continually," which went too far. They tightened up the statement that the King "has suffered the administration of justice totally to cease in some of these states by refusing his assent to laws for establishing judiciary powers," so it said he "obstructed the administration of justice by refusing his assent . . ." The complaint, remember, was mainly North Carolina's, so the reference to "some of these states" served curiously not to modify the charge but to reduce its accuracy. And the administration of justice there had not "totally" ceased since a political compromise allowed the inferior courts to continue functioning; only the superior courts were closed. The revised text was nearer the truth.

The delegates took the "our" out of the charge that the King had made "our judges dependent on his will alone," perhaps again for accuracy's sake. Judges, after all, had been Crown appointees, and so servants of the King. The delegates also cut the words "and ships of war" from the charge that the King had kept armies in the colonies without the permission of their legislatures, probably because the jurisdiction of those legislatures over the sea was open to dispute. In the end, the King stood accused of depriving the colonists of trial by jury "in many cases," not universally; he was not charged with withdrawing governors who had in fact often been forced from office, and he was said simply to have abdicated government by declaring the colonists "out of his protection"—which recalled the Prohibitory Act—"and waging war against us."

Above all, however, the delegates eliminated entirely Jefferson's long passage on the slave trade. In the notes he kept of Congress's proceedings, Jefferson said that change was made "in complaisance to South Carolina & Georgia," which had never tried to restrain the slave trade and, indeed, wanted it to continue, with the consent of "Northern brethren" who had few slaves but were sensitive on the issue because they had been "pretty considerable carriers of them to others."[5] Maybe so, but the very acknowledgment that colonists had been in the past or were at present willing participants in the slave trade undermined the assertion that "the *Christian* king of Great Britain" was alone responsible for that outrage on humanity. The Americans were destined to receive criticism enough for asserting the "inalienable" rights to "life, liberty, and the pursuit of happiness" while themselves owning slaves. Some people recognized the contradiction and were ready to move toward greater consistency between principle and practice, but so monumental a change as the abolition of slavery could not be accomplished in a moment. For the time being, it was wise at least not to call attention to the persistence of the slave trade and to the anomaly of American slavery.

The delegates did not, however, eliminate all reference to Lord Dunmore's effort to turn slaves against their masters, which, as the state and local resolutions testified, had powerfully alienated many colonists from

British rule, and to which Jefferson referred at the end of his long passage on the slave trade. After omitting that charge and another, which accused the King of inciting "treasonable insurrections of our fellow citizens," the delegates inserted into the seventeenth charge, which castigated the King for turning Indians against the people of the frontiers, an accusation that he had "excited domestic insurrections among us," which covered both slaves and Loyalists. The final Declaration therefore included not twenty-one but nineteen charges against the King — surely enough to demonstrate a "long train of abuses" and a "history of repeated injuries." Moreover, having eliminated the old eighteenth charge on "treasonable insurrections" with its reference to "our fellow citizens," the delegates were free to use that phrase in place of "others" in the next charge, so the King was accused of constraining "our fellow citizens taken captive [Jefferson had said "captives"] on the high seas to bear arms against their country. . . ."

By then the delegates seem to have built up steam, and really ripped into the rest of the document. And, indeed, it badly needed editing; Jefferson had probably lacked time to work over the final portions of the document with the same care he devoted to its opening. His reference to the Americans as "a people who mean to be free" became "a free people." Much better: Jefferson's words suggested that Americans aspired to freedom but were not yet free, which was far from the general sense of their situation, and had a certain unfortunate petulant tone as well. Then out went the strained assertion that "future ages will scarce believe" that one man had "in only twelve years" attempted to found so "broad and undisguised" a foundation for tyranny over a people "fostered and fixed in principles of freedom." Again, less was more.

On that same principle, Congress reduced Jefferson's overlong attack on the British people to a more lean and constrained statement. Out went his claim that the Americans had settled the country without any British help; the remaining assertion that "we reminded them of the circumstances of our emigration and settlement here" then became more justifiable. From the beginning of the conflict, the colonists had insisted that in coming to America their ancestors had yielded none of the rights of Englishmen. That could be construed as reminding the British people of the "circumstances of our emigration." Out went the detailed references to the British people's returning the parliamentary "disturbers of our harmony" to power and to their allowing the King to send mercenaries "to invade and destroy us." It was enough to say that they proved "deaf to the voice of justice and consanguinity," and that "we must therefore acquiesce in the necessity which denounces our separation" — cutting out the "eternal" before "separation" — to which the delegates added, "and hold them, as we hold the rest of mankind, enemies in war, in peace friends." Those words were Jefferson's, but their grace was lost in his own draft, buried as they were in the midst of false stops and restartings.

This was no hack editing job: the delegates who labored over the draft Declaration had a splendid ear for language. Jefferson, however, did not see it that way. The changes in the passages on the British people were made, he said, because "the pusillanimous idea that we had friends in England still keeping terms with, still haunted the minds of many."[6] But the rewritten section remained severely critical of the British people. The language, however, was more restrained, the conclusion more eloquent, and the whole more in keeping with the economy of Jefferson's opening paragraphs.

Finally, Congress substituted the words of its own July 2 resolution — the composition of another Virginian, Richard Henry Lee — for much of Jefferson's conclusion, and eliminated his troubling suggestion, so out of keeping with the increasingly orthodox American conception of the Empire as a collection of otherwise independent communities bound together under the Crown, that the Americans might once have had a more direct political connection with the people or Parliament of Britain. It also added two references to God, which were conspicuously missing in Jefferson's draft, where God appeared only as the author of nature's laws and the endower of natural rights, and honor alone was "sacred." At the start of the final paragraph Congress inserted an appeal "to the supreme judge of the world" to affirm "the rectitude of our intentions," which echoed similar provisions in several state and local resolutions on Independence, and nearer the end of the document it also referred to the delegates' "firm reliance on the protection of divine providence." Americans held strong religious beliefs in 1776, and the Declaration was meant to state the convictions of the country's "good people." The delegates retained, however, Jefferson's concluding sentences, including its memorable mutual pledge of "our lives, our fortunes, and our sacred honor."

The more alterations Congress made on his draft, the more miserable Jefferson became. He had forgotten, as has posterity, that a draftsman is not an author, and that the "declaration on independence," as Congress sometimes called it, was not a novel, or a poem, or even a political essay presented to the world as the work of a particular writer, but a public document, an authenticated expression of the American mind. Franklin, who was sitting nearby, "perceived that I was not insensible to these mutilations," Jefferson later recalled, and attempted to console him with the story of a young hatter, about to open his own shop, who proposed to have a fine signboard made with the words "John Thompson, Hatter, makes and sells hats for ready money" and the figure of a hat. First, however, he asked his friends for their advice. One proposed taking out "hatter" since it was redundant with "makes hats." Another recommended that "makes" be removed since customers wouldn't care who exactly made the hats. A third said "for ready money" was unnecessary since it was not the local custom to sell on credit. "*Sells* hats," a fourth commented; did Thompson suppose people thought he meant to give them away? In the end, the sign said simply "John Thompson," with a picture of a hat, which probably served its function quite well. Franklin said, however, that he had learned from that anecdote to avoid, "whenever in my power, . . . becoming the draughtsman of papers to be reviewed by a public body."[7] Did Franklin understand how much Congress, like the relentless editors in his story, was practicing a technique that Jefferson had himself used to good effect when he compressed Mason's language until it gained in power far more than it lost in length?

Others seem to have shared Jefferson's preference for the committee draft over the version Congress adopted. So strong was his conviction on that issue that Jefferson laboriously copied the earlier version several times over — by hand, of course, which made it a tedious, time-consuming task — and sent those copies to friends so they could judge for themselves, as he wrote Richard Henry Lee, "whether it is the better or worse for the Critics." Lee responded that he "sincerely" wished, "as well for the honor of Congress, as for that of the States, that the Manuscript had not been mangled as it is," and years later John Adams also said that Congress "obliterated some of the best" of the draft declaration "and left all that was exceptionable, if any thing in it was."[8] Obviously the two versions were strikingly different in the opinion of contemporary observers. And what generations of Americans came to revere was not Jefferson's but Congress's Declaration, the work not of a single man, or even a committee, but of a larger body of men with the good sense to recognize a "pretty good" draft when they saw it, and who were able to identify and eliminate Jefferson's more outlandish assertions and unnecessary words. So successful an exercise of group editing probably demanded a text that required cutting, not extensive rewriting. Congress's achievement was remarkable nonetheless. By exercising their intelligence, political good sense, and a discerning sense of language, the delegates managed to make the Declaration at once more accurate and more consonant with the convictions of their constituents, and to enhance both its power and its eloquence.

Finally, on July 4, the Committee of the Whole reported that it had agreed upon a Declaration. Congress's journal says that the text was then read and that Congress accepted it, ordered it to be authenticated and printed under the supervision of the drafting committee, and provided for its distribution and proclamation.[9] Jefferson's notes on Congress's proceedings for once added more detail. After devoting "the greater parts of the 2d. 3d. & 4th. July" in debating the declaration, he said, those deliberations were finally "in the evening of the last closed. the declaration was reported by the comm[itt]ee, agreed to by the house, and signed by every member present except Mr. Dickinson."[10] Careful research has been devoted to determining when exactly the Declaration was approved — late morning, not evening, seems most likely[11] — and whether the document was in fact signed on the 4th by anyone except Congress's President, John Hancock, whose name appeared as the sole signer on the published broadside. There remains a remote possibility that delegates signed a copy of the Declaration that has since been lost, but probably Jefferson was wrong there, too.[12] The Journals of the Second Continental Congress say only that on July 19, after New York's approval became known, Congress resolved "that the Declaration passed on the 4th, be fairly engrossed on parchment, with the title and stile of 'The unanimous declaration of the thirteen United States of America,' and that the same, when engrossed, be signed by every member of Congress," and that on August 2 "the declaration of independence being engrossed and compared was signed,"[13] although some members added their signatures at later times.

Why, however, was it signed at all? Only John Browne, Parliament's clerk, signed the English Declaration of Rights. Moreover, according to Lois Schwoerer, the members of England's seventeenth-century Parliaments did not customarily sign instruments they presented to the King, nor were declarations and petitions signed by their drafters elsewhere in Europe. "Of documents comparable to the Declaration of Rights," she says, "only the Declaration of Independence of the American colonies was signed by its framers."[14]

The Declaration of Independence was not the only Congressional document that was signed by the delegates. Members of the First Continental Congress had affixed their signatures to the Continental Association and to their petition to the King, but not to the addresses they sent the inhabitants of Great Britain and of the American colonies, "The Bill of Rights [and] a List of Grievances," or, finally, their letter to the inhabitants of Quebec, which was simply signed "By order of the Congress, Henry Middleton, President," on October 26, 1774. The Second Continental Congress signed its "Olive Branch Petition" to the King but no other document previous to the Declaration of Independence, although some were, again, signed by John Hancock as President of the Congress.[15]

In the absence of any direct testimony on why some documents were signed and others not, the answer or answers to that riddle must lie in the texts themselves. The Association set up a colony-wide nonimportation, nonexportation, and nonconsumption agreement. Since the First Continental Congress had no independent legislative authority, the document's binding character could come only from the consent of those who were parties to it. The text made that clear and also mandated that delegates sign: ". . . we do solemnly bind ourselves and our constituents," it said, ". . . to adhere to this association. . . ." The signing of petitions to the King, contrary as it was to Parliamentary practice, is somewhat more difficult to explain. Again, the documents were written in a way that made delegates' signatures necessary. "We your majesty's faithful subjects of the colonies of Newhampshire, Massachusetts-by, Rhode-island and Providence Plantations, Connecticut, New-York, New-Jersey, Pennsylvania, the counties of New-Castle Kent and Sussex on Delaware, Maryland, Virginia, North-Carolina, and South Carolina," began the petition of 1774, "in behalf of ourselves and the inhabitants of these colonies who have deputed us to represent them in General Congress, by this our humble petition, beg leave to lay our grievances before the throne." Its successor of 1775 began in an almost identical way, except that the opening statement entreated "your Majesty's gracious attention to this our humble petition."[16]

But why were the petitions written in that way? Probably out of respect for the King, and to enhance the petitions' persuasiveness. Unlike the convention Parliament of 1689, Congress had no place in British constitutional tradition. It was new, and the Crown did not recognize its legitimacy. By affixing their signatures, the delegates signaled that each of the colonies mentioned supported the petition, and also founded it upon their own personal authority and dignity. This was, they seemed to say, not the work of an inconsequential faction of colonists, as their critics in England so often alleged, but the voice of the American people and of the men of consequence they selected to speak for them. Since, moreover, the petitions were conspicuously loyal statements from the King's "faithful subjects," there was no particular reason not to sign.

The Declaration of Independence was altogether different. It was not loyal; it was an avowal of revolution. From the viewpoint of those who opposed its message, the Declaration was nothing less than a public confession of treason. And conviction for treason meant death and confiscation of estate. Surely there was cause enough for fear: opponents in England had long since begun urging the King to prosecute the colonists for treason. In 1776, the supporters of Independence suspected that some colonies had adopted a "settled policy to keep in the rear of the confederacy, that their particular prospect might be better even in the worst event."[17]

Signing the Declaration was no way "to keep in the rear." Nonetheless, the delegates adopted a document that, like the Association, and like the petitions to the King, mandated their signatures. "We, therefore, the Representatives of the United states of America," it concluded, ". . . do, in the name, and by the authority of the good people of these Colonies, solemnly publish and declare, that these united colonies are, and of right ought to be free and independent States." By eliminating from his draft conspicuous debts to the English Declaration of Rights, Jefferson had constructed a document that manifested the Independence it declared. In the same way, the signers, by affixing their names to the text, and so making their signatures part of that most hazardous of Congressional papers, mutually pledged to each other, "for the support of this Declaration" and "with a firm reliance on the protection of divine Providence," their lives, their fortunes, and their sacred honor.

They were not, however, given to throwing their fate into God's hands needlessly. Only on January 18, 1777, after the long, disastrous military campaign of 1776 was over and the Americans had won victories at Trenton and Princeton, did Congress send the states authenticated copies of the Declaration of Independence "with the names of the members . . . subscribing the same."[18]

Notes

1. Worthington Chauncey Ford, ed., *Journals of the Continental Congress, 1774–1789* [JCC] (5 vols., Washington, D.C., 1904–06), V: 507.

2. Ibid., 507, 510.

3. Wilfred J. Ritz, "From the *Here* of Jefferson's Handwritten Rough Draft of the Declaration of Independence to the *There* of the Printed Dunlap Broadside," the *Pennsylvania Magazine of History & Biography*, CXVI (1992), 499–512. Ritz also argues that a printed fragment of the Declaration at the Historical Society of Pennsylvania, which earlier scholars described as a "proof" for the broadside published by John Dunlap after Congress approved the Declaration, was in fact "a distinct printing . . . made between the (now lost) first printing of Jefferson's draft Declaration and the final printing known as the *Dunlap Broadside*" (504).

4. Bartlett to John Langdon, Philadelphia, July 1, 1776, in Paul H. Smith, ed., *Letters of Delegates to Congress, 1774–1789* [LDC] (4 vols., Washington, D.C. [Library of Congress], 1976–79), IV: 351. The discussion that follows draws upon the version of the document in Carl Becker, *The Declaration of Independence: A Study in the History of Political Ideas* (1922; New York, 1942), 174–84, which shows the changes Congress made in the committee draft, and the slightly amended rendition of the document as Becker presented it below, in Appendix C [not included in the present volume].

5. Julian P. Boyd, ed., *The Papers of Thomas Jefferson,* (Princeton, 1950), I: 314–15.

6. Ibid., 314.

7. Printed with Jefferson's letter to Robert Walsh, Monticello, December 4, 1818, in Paul Leicester Ford, ed., *The Writings of Thomas Jefferson* (New York and London, 1899), X: 120n.

8. Lee to Jefferson, Chantilly (his plantation in Virginia), July 21, 1776, in Boyd I: 471; Adams to Pickering, August 6, 1822, in Charles Francis Adams, ed., *The Works of John Adams* (Boston, 1850), II: 514n.

9. JCC V: 510–16.

10. Boyd I: 315.

11. Cf. LDC IV, editorial note at 381–82.

12. The cases for and against a signing on July 4 are summarized in Boyd I: 304–08, which also refers to other discussions of the subject.

13. JCC V: 590–91, 626. The copy reprinted, with signatures, under the entry for July 4 on pp. 510–15 was taken from "the engrossed original in the Department of State," and so is of a later date. A printed broadside from Congress's "Rough Journal" is reproduced in Julian P. Boyd, *The Declaration of Independence: The Evolution of the Text as Shown in Facsimiles of Various Drafts by Its Author* (Washington, D.C.: 1943), plate X.

14. Lois G. Schwoerer, *The Declaration of Rights, 1689* (Baltimore and London, 1981), 13.

15. James H. Hutson, ed., *A Decent Respect to the Opinions of Mankind: Congressional State Papers, 1774–1776* (Washington, D.C., 1975), passim.

16. Ibid., 13, 75, 127.

17. On invocations of 35 Henry VIII, c. 2, with regard to treason or misprision of treason committed outside the realm, see *Decent Respect,* p. 32, n. 8; Jefferson's notes on Congress's proceedings in Boyd I: 312.

18. John Hazelton, *The Declaration of Independence: Its History* (New York, 1906), 284.

Making Connections

The questions that precede each selection are intended to help students deal with a particular piece of writing. But all the selections here are in dialogue with one another around one larger problem. That problem is how we can best understand the founding moment of the United States, as expressed in the Declaration of Independence. As the selections show, there are many possibilities for addressing that problem. They may be mutually exclusive. Or they may complement one another. It is certainly the case that each of these selections makes much more sense if it is read as part of a discussion rather than standing alone. The questions that follow should aid students to realize that the discussion is not finished and that everyone is free to join in.

1. Does the scholarly approach toward the Declaration undermine its status as a source of American mythology?

2. What legal standing, if any, does the Declaration have in our national history?

3. Is the Declaration finally a liberal or radical statement? Was it written as a propagandistic rationalization of American interests or a sincere expression of American ideals?

4. Should we think of the ideas in the Declaration as timeless truths or as products of a particular movement in history? Can they be both?

5. How do the different selections address the deletion of Jefferson's slavery passage? Do the different approaches represent the different times in which authors lived and worked or do they suggest nuances in our understanding of the problem of slavery in revolutionary America?

6. Reread both Jefferson's draft of the Declaration and Congress's final version. How do the five secondary sources help you understand the differences between these two texts?

7. How do the arguments about influences on the Declaration's writing change your understanding of such key phrases as, "all men are created equal" and "life, liberty, and the pursuit of happiness"?

8. What do you now think we are celebrating each Fourth of July? Do we have the date right?

Suggestions for Further Reading

This volume is not intended to provide a massive bibliography, but any interested student will want to delve into the subject more deeply. For a selection drawn from a book, the best way to start is to go to that book and place the selection within the author's larger argument. Each selection is reproduced with full annotation, as originally published, to allow interested students to go to the author's original sources, study them, and compare their own readings with what the author has made of the same material.

The authoritative study of the textual history of the Declaration is Julian P. Boyd, *The Declaration of Independence: The Evolution of the Text* (Washington, D.C.: Library of Congress, 1943). The classic argument for the Declaration as a Lockean document is Carl Becker, *The Declaration of Independence: A Study in the History of Political Ideas* (New York: Harcourt, Brace, 1922). The case for the Scottish influence is made by Garry Wills, *Inventing America: Jefferson's Declaration of Independence* (Garden City, N.Y.: Doubleday, 1978). The best appraisal of the Becker–Wills debate is Ronald Hamowy, "Jefferson and the Scottish Enlightenment: A Critique of Garry Will's *Inventing America*," *William and Mary Quarterly*, 3rd Series, XXXVI (October 1979), 503–23. A distinctive argument that Jefferson wrote the Declaration to be read aloud, so it should be studied as a piece of rhetoric, is Jay Fliegelman, *Declaring Independence: Jefferson, Natural Language and the Culture of Performance* (Stanford, Calif.: Stanford University Press, 1993).

The clearest statement of the Neo-Whig interpretation of the American Revolution is Edmund S. Morgan, *The Challenge of the American Revolution* (New York: Norton, 1976). The seminal study of revolutionary ideology is Bernard Bailyn, *The Ideological Origins of the American Revolution* (Cambridge, Mass.: Belknap Press of Harvard University Press, 1967). The strongest case for the transformative power of the revolutionary ideology is Gordon S. Wood, *The Radicalism of the American Revolution* (New York: Knopf, 1992). The authoritative account of the Continental Congress is Jack N. Rakove, *The Beginnings of National Politics: An Interpretive History of the Continental Congress* (New York: Knopf, 1979). The most recent assessment of Thomas Jefferson is my *American Sphinx: The Character of Thomas Jefferson* (New York: Knopf, 1997). The best book-length treatment of the drafting, editing, and impact of the Declaration is Pauline Maier, *American Scripture: Making the Declaration of Independence* (New York: Knopf, 1997).

On the subsequent history of the Declaration in the postrevolutionary years, see Philip Detweiler, "The Changing Reputation of the Declaration of Independence: The First Fifty Years," *William and Mary Quarterly*, 3rd Series, XIX (1962), 557–74. A more comprehensive view of the evolution in the Declaration's meaning is Merrill D. Peterson, *The Jefferson Image in the American Mind* (New York: Oxford University Press, 1960).